Global Outlook
High Intermediate Reading

Brenda Bushell and Brenda Dyer

Global Outlook 2

Published by McGraw-Hill/Contemporary, a business unit of The McGraw-Hill Companies, Inc., 1221 Avenue of the Americas, New York, NY 10020. Copyright © 2003 by The McGraw-Hill Companies, Inc. All rights reserved. No part of this publication may be reproduced or distributed in any form or by any means, or stored in a database or retrieval system, without the prior written consent of The McGraw-Hill Companies, Inc., including, but not limited to, in any network or other electronic storage or transmission, or broadcast for distance learning.

 This book is printed on recycled, acid-free paper containing 10% postconsumer waste.

3 4 5 6 7 8 9 0 DOC 0 9 8 7 6 5 4

ISBN 0-07-250325-4

Editorial director: *Tina Carver*
Sponsoring editor: *Thomas Healy*
Cover image: © *Leon Zernitsky*

TABLE OF CONTENTS

INTRODUCTION

Global Outlook 2 is designed to introduce advanced learners of English as a Foreign or Second Language to the basic reading skills required for fluent, accurate reading in English.

Global Outlook 2 is the second book in a two-level series. The key features of the *Global Outlook* series are high-interest content, careful sequencing of reading skills, and oral communication extension activities which encourage students to go beyond the reading text and consider how the issues impact their lives.

Students will:

- Acquire reading skills which fluent readers of English use unconsciously

- Learn to use their background knowledge to understand a text

- Develop the ability to read chunks of information for general understanding instead of reading and translating word-for-word

- Expand their knowledge and build a global perspective of world issues and social trends.

Global Outlook is designed for both teachers who are experienced in teaching reading skills but looking for new ways to implement them, and those who are less experienced and are looking for guidance on how to incorporate specific reading-skill development in their language classes.

➤ APPROACHES TO TEACHING READING

One of the keys to teaching reading effectively is to present high-interest, provocative reading material which will engage the reader. The readings have been carefully chosen to include a variety of viewpoints on global topics centered around social issues, the environment, psychology, business, and technology. The readings also include various styles: journalism (newspaper and magazines), interviews, advertisements, fiction, poetry, and academic essays. The readings, though diverse, share the common theme of global content. Vocabulary and concepts related to global education are recycled throughout the text, building up a basic core of knowledge. When topics are integrated rather than randomly presented, general comprehension is facilitated.

Reading skills are carefully presented and practiced. One of the common stumbling blocks for second and foreign-language students is their use of "bottom-up" information processing, that is, word-by-word translation of the text for comprehension. This is not efficient and often leads to slow, inaccurate reading. *Global Outlook* emphasizes the top-down reading process, in which the reader uses what he or she already knows in trying to comprehend the text. Pre-reading exercises, finding the main idea, and vocabulary in context exercises are examples of how this textbook reinforces efficient top-down reading strategies.

The skills of the reading process are articulated for the student in each unit. Research shows that it is possible to divide reading into a series of sub-processes and students can be trained in specific reading comprehension skills which they can transfer to new reading situations. Students learn about the reading process itself, and begin to realize that "reading" is not the same thing as "translating." Skill-focus highlights the thinking processes which good English readers use in understanding a text in English. This meta-cognitive awareness is an important basis for language acquisition in adult learners. Therefore, the *process* of comprehending should be the purpose of each unit.

➤ UNIT ORGANIZATION

The following exercises are included in each unit. The sequence of exercises may vary from unit to unit, depending on the reading skill which is targeted.

Before You Begin: In this section, students are asked to think about the topic of the reading, and make predictions. By previewing, students recall information to begin the cognitive process of matching new information with what is already known. This enhances reading comprehension not only by sparking interest, but by building content and vocabulary schema.

Getting the Main Idea: This is an important top-down reading skill that requires students to actively process global information as they read, without getting distracted by details. Students learn to use the pre-reading information they have gathered from the Before You Begin section to access the main point of the reading while reading for the first time. Rhetorical strategies for locating the main idea are especially targeted in Unit 4, but practice for this very important skill is given in each unit.

Vocabulary in Context: One of the most important reading skills of this text is the ability to guess the meaning of unknown words from context. Students often depend on their dictionaries too much, which slows down their reading speed and interferes with comprehension. Using cues such as grammatical and semantic context, punctuation, and transitions, students can become confident in inferring the meaning of key words. In order for this exercise to be effective, students must NOT use their dictionaries.

Reading Skill: One particular reading skill is targeted in each unit. Each reading is accompanied by a specific reading skill description and exercise. These reading skills are unconscious in fluent English readers, but they can be learned. By becoming aware of these reading processes, students will become more effective readers.

Taking a Closer Look: The ability to find important information is developed through the practice of scanning. Students learn how to search quickly to extract certain specific information without reading through the whole text. For academic English, scanning is absolutely essential. In vocational or daily English, scanning is useful in dealing with schedules, manuals, forms, and other list-oriented reading genres.

Communicate: One of the unique features of this reading text is that the reading is supported by speaking. Each unit is followed by a "Communicate" speaking activity. In the speaking activity, students are given a chance to personalize the text, that is, make connections between the readings and their own lives and opinions. It is a good opportunity to recycle unit vocabulary. For teachers concerned with values education, this section gives students a chance to develop their opinions of the ideas presented in the readings and also raises their awareness of the diversity of values and beliefs of their classmates. Finally, when students realize that this is a post-reading component of each unit, they tend to approach the readings more critically, forming judgments and opinions of the content they will share with their classmates. In other words, it becomes a built-in motivator for reading.

Interactive Journal Response: These final questions provide another chance for vocabulary recycling, and closure for each unit. Students are asked to interpret the information of the reading, give their opinions, and respond. We have chosen provocative topics which we hope students will respond to by agreeing or disagreeing. One of the purposes of the text is to empower students to become independent, critical thinkers and readers. The instruction is for students to choose one question and write a response. This could be collected by teachers as a check of reading comprehension. The other option is for students to paraphrase their response orally with a partner or in small groups, in the following class as a warm-up activity. The exercise is not intended to be a formal writing exercise, but rather a final communicative activity to support the students' reading comprehension. If students feel that their reactions to and opinions of the readings are valued, their motivation for reading future units will be enhanced.

THE MILLENNIAL GENERATION

I n this chapter you will consider your generation's place in history. The 21st century brings complex systems, possibilities, and problems. It is said that the people born between the years 1980 and 2000 have a special role to play in these confusing but exciting times. The Millennial Generation embraces change and looks to the new century with courage and curiosity.

READING ONE

➤ BEFORE YOU BEGIN

Part A

With your partner, make a list of:

- 5 problems facing the world today (for example, air pollution).

- 5 useful or interesting things about the world today (for example, airplanes).

- 5 things, good or bad, that you predict will happen in the future.

Share your ideas with the class.

Part B

In this chapter you will be working on your reading pace by practicing the skill of skimming. First, follow these steps:

1. Circle the title.

2. <u>Underline</u> the first sentence and last sentence of the first paragraph.

3. Underline the first sentence of each paragraph.

4. Underline the first sentence and last sentence of the last paragraph.

Now skim: Read what you underlined and let your eyes move quickly over the rest of the passage. A good reading pace for the first time is about 800 words per minute, so give yourself one and a half minutes to skim the passage.

Based on your skimming, what seems to be the main topic of the reading?

a. _____ problems and limitations of young people these days

b. _____ important changes in the 21st century

c. _____ positive characteristics of young people these days

➤ AS YOU READ

Now read "The Millennial Generation" again to get a more complete idea.

THE MILLENNIAL GENERATION
by Deborah Jones, from *The Globe and Mail*

1   At Point Grey Mini-School in Vancouver, Canada, teenagers discuss a subject that fully engages them: Their generation's place in history. "We're totally different" says Rafal, a Grade 9 student. "We're the first to grow up with a lot of technology around us. It changes our perspective." Says his classmate Campbell: "We have much more   5
information access. We are the first group to have sex education in Grade 3." Aged 14 and 15, these teens feel an important sense of duty to fix problems left behind by older generations, principally by their Baby Boomer parents. High on the list of problems is repairing the destruction of the environment passed on so carelessly to them.   10

2   A generation is composed of people whose common location in history gives them a common viewpoint and personality. Sociologists and researchers of demographics[1] have divided the 20th century into five "generations," each with its own characteristics.

Name	Years	Characteristics
GI[2]	1901–1924	altruistic[3], idealistic
Silent	1925–1942	lost generation, disillusioned[4]
Baby Boomer	1943–1960	me first
Generation X	1961–1980	cynical[5], pessimistic
Millennial	1981–2003	altruistic, globally minded

3   According to researchers, the North American kids born in the last   15
20 years—the so-called Millennial Generation—will be a troop of "good Scouts"[6] who, as they mature, will insist on solutions to an accumulation of society's problems and injustices. They will aim to fix the environmental destruction left behind by their parents, the well-intentioned but me-first Baby Boomers. These children are   20
expected to be much more cooperative and socially involved than the Boomers. Weaned on technological, social, and economic change,

---

[1] *demographics:* scientific study of population statistics
[2] *GI:* an enlisted person in the US army
[3] *altruistic:* unselfish
[4] *disillusioned:* set free from pleasant but mistaken beliefs
[5] *cynical:* pessimistic; believing people's motives are bad
[6] *"good Scouts":* referring to Boy Scouts who promise to do their best to help others

their impatience and drive will very likely shake the world and its institutions, including schools and universities.

4   Some demographers, such as authors Neil Howe and William Strauss, compare the Millennial Generation to the GI Generation born before the Second World War, during 1901–24, the generation of John F. Kennedy who said, "Ask not what your country can do for you, but what you can do for your country." Howe and Strauss predict that, like the GIs four generations before them, the Millennials will be willing to lay down their lives for causes they consider right and just. They will fight for democracy, rescue the environment, and develop alternative sources of energy. They will be leaders in debates about genetic engineering and biotechnology, basic human rights, economic fairness in an emerging global economy, and closing the digital divide[7]. They will embrace diversity, question materialism, and have new visions for career and work.

5   The world of the Millennial Generation is full of questions and uncertainty. Until now most North Americans grew up with some sense of the roles they would play as individuals, spouses, parents, workers, and consumers. But everything now seems fluid, unknown, from job expectations to gender identification. Most Millennials will not have one job for life, but will have to have a variety of skills for a variety of jobs. In the face of such uncertainty, what would cause the Millennials to be so optimistic? Why are they so altruistic, stable, and self-confident? One main answer, say theorists, is the shift to "family values" in the last twenty years. In the 1960s and 1970s, self-fulfillment was more important than family. Social historian Franki Gregorsky of Seattle Discovery Institute explains that Generation X children raised between 1961 and 1981 often appear negative with their harsh music, dark fashions and body piercing. But by the 1980s social values shifted back to the importance of family. Even though families recently seem more hard-pressed than ever to make ends meet and find time for one another, divorce rates in North America have stopped climbing. Howe credits the Baby Boomer parents and their intense interest in child rearing and education. Even though the parenting itself may have been egocentric, with the view of producing the "perfect child," the result is

---

[7] *digital divide:* the gap between countries that have access to technology and those that don't

positive thinkers who tackle challenges with confidence and reject the emotional and material self-indulgence of the previous generation. This generation of kids has been nurtured, protected, and valued, and they have strong values themselves.

6   But don't think that the Millennial Generation will bring an age of sunshine and sweetness! Skeptics point out the widening gap between the haves and have-nots throughout Canada and the US, especially in inner cities. Youth crime is up. The number of children living in poverty throughout North America has increased. Even in relatively rich families, many children lack adequate adult care because both parents work long hours. The good Scouts will likely be confined to families with thoughtful parents and access to good education, health care, and technologies like home computers.

7   One difference between the Millennial Generation and those that came before is the unprecedented globalization of society and the economy. This seems most obvious in young people's individual awareness of themselves as part of a larger community and their responsibility to improve it. The children at Point Grey Mini-School, Vancouver, are vivid examples of this. They are at the leading edge of change driven by technology. The children do research on the Internet and have progressed into a whole new way of using it. They carry out self-directed research on the Internet on topics of their choice. Then, instead of simply writing essays, as previous generations did, they "web out" from a central idea to create web pages, make videos, and write articles for school projects.

8   Partly because of a global perspective, these representatives of the Millennial Generation are much better prepared for the future. They are able to relate to one another with less racism and sexism than earlier generations. As well as being positive, they are well aware of the global economy, more able to get along with different people, and quite comfortable with a lack of job security.

►GETTING THE MAIN IDEA

The author's main idea is:

a. _____ The Millennial Generation has its own characteristics, which include an interest in solving social and global problems.

b. _____ The Millennial Generation is facing an uncertain and troubled future, and doesn't know how to cope.

c. _____ The changes of today's world are happening too fast, and the Millennial Generation is suffering a lot of stress due to the speed of change.

►READING SKILL: Reading Pace

Reading pace refers to how quickly you read. Often second language students read English slowly and carefully and use their dictionaries constantly. This is one way of reading, but it is not always the best way. You can improve your reading pace by skipping unknown words. It is not always good to interrupt your reading to check the dictionary. It is not necessary to understand every word in order to understand a sentence or a reading passage. In fact, it is a useful reading strategy to read quickly, skipping unknown words, and focusing on the main ideas.

To improve your reading pace, you should practice skimming and skipping unknown words.

1. In *Before You Begin* at the beginning of this unit, you skimmed through the passage very quickly, noticing the title and the first sentence of each paragraph. This is a good first step.

2. After skimming to get the general idea, it is helpful to go back and read the passage a second time, still keeping up a fast pace, but reading a little more carefully. Skip the unknown words.

➤ READING SKILL PRACTICE: Reading Pace

Read the following paragraph. It is the third paragraph from "The Millennial Generation," but every eighth word is missing. Just skip over the blanks and then try to answer the questions that follow.

According to researchers, the North American kids _____ in the last 20 years—the so-_____ Millennial Generation—will be a troop of "_____ Scouts" who, as they mature, will insist _____ solutions to an accumulation of society's problems _____ injustices. They will aim to fix the _____ destruction left behind by their parents, the _____ -intentioned but me-first Baby Boomers. These _____ are expected to be much more cooperative _____ socially involved than the boomers. Weaned on _____, social, and economic change, their impatience and _____ will very likely shake the world and _____ institutions, including schools and universities.

True or false?

1. _____ The Millennial Generation refers to North American children born in the last 20 years.

2. _____ These young people will ignore social problems.

3. _____ They are expected to be uncooperative social rebels.

4. _____ They will try to change the world.

After you have finished the questions, go back to the reading and read paragraph three again. Check your answers. Even with many unknown (missing) words, you were probably able to answer the questions correctly. You do not need to read or know every word in order to understand. Practicing skimming and skipping unknown words is one way to improve your reading pace. Remember: 800 words per minute is a good skimming rate. Practice reading the passages in this textbook very quickly the first and second times, trying to catch the general topic and organization of the reading. After that, you can go back and read more carefully. You will soon notice an improvement in your reading comprehension.

➤ VOCABULARY IN CONTEXT

The following sentences contain vocabulary from "The Millennial Generation."
Circle the best definition of the underlined word.

1. The boy was so <u>engaged</u> by the TV program that he forgot to eat his snack.

    a. interested

    b. bored

    c. ignored

2. He failed the class <u>principally</u> because of his poor attendance.

    a. even though

    b. mainly

    c. proudly

3. Because of the <u>accumulation</u> of papers in his office, he did not have any place to sit down.

    a. increased amount

    b. disappearance

    c. grading

4. The healthy cat <u>was weaned on fish</u>.

    a. was tired of fish

    b. got sick from fish

    c. ate fish as its first food

5. They hired her because of her <u>drive</u> to improve the company's image.

    a. rude behavior

    b. car

    c. ambition

6. The <u>self-indulgence</u> of the young mother bothered the wise old grandmother.

    a. beauty

    b. selfishness

    c. confidence

7. The dancer's movements were <u>fluid</u>.

   a. changing smoothly like water

   b. stiff and awkward

   c. strict

8. It was difficult for the young family <u>to make ends meet</u> every month.

   a. pay their bills

   b. meet their friends

   c. get enough sleep

9. Don't tell your plan to him. He's a <u>skeptic</u> and will try to discourage you.

   a. optimist

   b. person who doesn't believe in anything

   c. kind, supportive person

10. There was a big <u>gap</u> between the step and the ground, so she fell down.

   a. space

   b. connection

   c. understanding

➤ TAKING A CLOSER LOOK

Read "The Millennial Generation" again, focusing on details. Are these sentences true (**T**) or false (**F**)? Underline a sentence or phrase in the reading that supports your answer. Compare your answers with your classmates' answers.

1. _____ One reason the Millennial Generation is different is that they have grown up with a lot of technology and access to information.

2. _____ The Millennials are patient and accept the way things are.

3. _____ They are not willing to risk themselves for social causes.

4. _____ According to the author, John F. Kennedy would be a good spokesperson for the Millennials.

5. _____ The Millennials will not have one life-long career, but several different jobs.

6. _____ Baby Boomer parents were very committed to good child-rearing.

7. _____ The author admits that there are many problems facing young people of the Millennial Generation.

8. _____ Using the Internet has made students more dependent on the teacher, and less willing to try new ideas.

9. _____ The author claims that today's kids are not as racist or sexist as previous generations.

►COMMUNICATE

Part One: Opinion Survey

Find three classmates to speak to. Ask each of them their opinions on the following statements. Write their opinions in the chart. Use the expressions for Asking Opinions on page 211 to help you.

1. Racism and sexism are old-fashioned.

2. Money is the most important thing in life.

3. To have one job for life is necessary and important.

Opinion . . .	Classmate A Name:	Classmate B Name:	Classmate C Name:
On #1			
On #2			
On #3			
On #4			
On #5			

4. The digital divide is inevitable.

5. Social problems like world poverty are impossible to solve.

Part Two: Group Sharing

After you have finished the survey, sit down with a group of three or four and share the results of your survey.

Example: Tomoko said that she completely agreed with the first statement. In her opinion . . .

Use the expressions for Reporting Opinions on page 211 to help you.

➤ INTERACTIVE JOURNAL RESPONSE

Choose one of the following questions and write a response. Be prepared to give an oral summary.

1. Were you born during the years of the Millennial Generation? Do you consider yourself a Millennial? How are your attitudes similar to or different from those described in the reading as typical of Millennials?

2. Do you agree that the Millennial Generation has a global perspective? Do you? How is a global perspective expressed in the daily lives of young people today? Give examples.

CULTURAL
ENCOUNTERS

Culture is a way of life that a group of people shares: their customs, beliefs, values, and communication system. Living in a world where different cultures meet on a daily basis can sometimes be difficult, but if everyone makes an effort to become more sensitive to each other's culture, the experience can be positive.

READING ONE

➤**BEFORE YOU BEGIN**

1. When we first visit or live in a different culture from our own we are sometimes surprised at what we find. Sometimes the reality does not match our
   dreams or ideas of that place. Take a survey of your classmates. Use the
   chart below.

   Ask:

   a. What foreign country have you read about or visited?

   b. What surprised you most about the traditions or culture of that foreign
   country?

   Example:

Name	**Country visited**	**What surprised you?**
Mike	Japan	People don't shake hands.

Name	**Country visited**	**What surprised you?**

   When you finish, discuss your answers with a small group.

2. Use the reading skills you learned in Unit 1 to predict the contents of
   Reading One. Read the title and say what you think it means. Skim the first
   and last paragraphs. Based on your skimming, what do you think the reading is about?

   a. _____ what Chinese people think about Chinese-Americans

   b. _____ how Chinese-Americans are treated in China

   c. _____ how a Chinese-American discovers herself in China

➤ AS YOU READ

Now read "An American Finding Her Chinese Face" once, quickly. When you finish, look back at *Before You Begin*. Do you still agree with your answer to Question 2?

AN AMERICAN FINDING HER CHINESE FACE
by Wendy Lum, from *China Daily*

1   The first time I lived in China, I was amazed to see so many different Chinese faces; I never knew that there could be such a diversity of faces in a population that seemed so alike. I was so surprised to see such a difference. The ironic[1] part of all this was that I was one of those faces. You see, I am an overseas Chinese.

2   I had come to China to teach as a foreign teacher at a university in Guangzhuo. It seemed my lifelong dream of coming back to my "motherland" was being fulfilled. Yet I remembered that sooner or later I would have to open my mouth and my secret identity would be discovered.

3   My first experience of being questioned as to why I did not know any Chinese was when I went to get my bike fixed. "What?" said the bike repairman, "You are Chinese so you should know how to speak Chinese." I tried to explain in my limited Chinese (Cantonese) that in America, everyone speaks English and that unless you are fortunate enough to go to Chinese school, you speak only English. Somehow, I was unable to convince the bike repairman that I honestly wanted to be more in tune, more familiar with my Chinese side, but had never had that opportunity up until now.

4   You see, I grew up in the very diverse multi-cultural mix[2] of Hawaii, which is noted for being a melting pot—where cultures are

---

[1] *ironic:* an unexpected connection between things that seem unrelated
[2] *multi-cultural mix:* many cultures existing together smoothly

encouraged to blend together. Therefore, coming to China was a
cultural shock[3] for me. However, by the end of my first year in   30
China, not only had I mastered the language, but I was able to blend
in like a native[4]. To my delight, I was able to bargain things down to
almost half the price, order dishes at restaurants for my American
friends, and carry on a normal conversation with any one on the
street. I could also spit out bones on the table without worrying   35
whether it was bad manners or not, and I mastered the fine art of
biking around the congested streets with out getting hit, and eating
almost anything with no questions asked.

5   After returning to Hawaii for a year, I am now once again in
China to teach. Even though I sometimes feel more at home in   40
Hawaii, I am drawn to this country and feel the need to spend more
time here to discover who I really am. I sometimes ask myself why I
love China so much, despite my frustrations with trying to learn the
language and coming to terms with the culture. It is not clear to me
yet, but I'm here to look for answers. What I do know is that there   45
is an unexplained beauty about the land, culture, history and most
of all the people here.

6   Still, after all my enthusiasm and determination to fit into this culture, some things have not changed. My students still think I am
Japanese, and they are incredulous (totally in disbelief) that I write 50
with my left hand. I am still struggling to learn the language, this
time Mandarin instead of Cantonese. I find that at times I really
identify with my Chinese side and at other times, my American.
Perhaps that is how things will always be, that I will be forever
caught between two worlds.   55

---

[3] *cultural shock*: feeling of anxiety someone has when visiting a new country
[4] *native*: someone who was born in an area or country

➤ GETTING THE MAIN IDEA

The author's main idea is:

a. _____ Life in China is not the same as life in Hawaii.

b. _____ Defining your cultural identity can be difficult.

c. _____ Foreign people have a lot of trouble in Chinese society.

➤ READING SKILL: Vocabulary in Context

Part A: Guessing Meaning from Context

The skill of learning to guess the general meaning of unknown words from the context of the sentence or paragraph will help you become a faster, more effective reader. To learn this skill, try reading without using a dictionary. When you come across an unfamiliar word, don't rely on your dictionary, but try to gather information from the surrounding words and sentences to help you get a general understanding of its meaning.

Here is an example of guessing the meaning from context. Read these sentences from Paragraph 1 and the explanation that follows.

Sentences from Paragraph 1

*I never knew that there could be such a **diversity** of faces in a population that seemed so alike. I was so surprised to see such a difference.*

Explanation

It is not hard to guess the meaning of the word **diversity**. Perhaps you don't know the exact definition, but there is enough information from the surrounding words to help you to make an intelligent guess. It you had to pick one of the following words as being similar in meaning to **diversity**, which would you pick?

  a. small number   **b.** variety   **c.** sameness

Yes, the answer is *variety*. The sentence tells us the author thought the Chinese population would be alike but she was surprised to see such a difference. By studying the surrounding context clues we can imagine the general meaning.

Sometimes, of course, it is necessary to use your dictionary; for example, when there is not enough context in the sentence or paragraph for you to make a good guess, or if you are taking a vocabulary test on the TOEFL, or when you are using a word in your own speaking or writing. But in general reading, checking every unknown word in the dictionary not only slows you down; it makes you lose the general meaning of what you are reading. It also makes you less confident about using your intelligence and imagination.

➤ READING SKILL PRACTICE: Guessing Meaning from Context

Without a dictionary, use the context of the sentence to guess the meaning of each <u>underlined</u> word. Write a synonym or definition for each word. Then use a dictionary to check your answers. The first one is done as an example.

1. I was <u>amazed</u> to see so many Chinese faces. I never knew there could be such a diversity.

    Your explanation: _surprised_

    Dictionary: _astonished, surprised_

2. I remembered that sooner or later I would have to open my mouth and my secret <u>identity</u> would be discovered.

    Your explanation: _____

    Dictionary: _____

3. I tried to explain in my limited Chinese that in America, everyone speaks English and that unless you are <u>fortunate</u> enough to go to Chinese school, you speak only English.

    Your explanation: _____

    Dictionary: _____

4. I mastered the fine art of biking around the <u>congested</u> streets without getting hit by the many bicycles and cars.

    Your explanation: _____

    Dictionary: _____

5. I sometimes ask myself why I love China so much, despite my <u>frustrations</u> with trying to learn the language and coming to terms with the culture.

    Your explanation: _____

    Dictionary: _____

6. I am still <u>struggling</u> to learn the language, this time Mandarin instead of Cantonese.

    Your explanation: _____

    Dictionary: _____

Part B: Contextual Paraphrasing by Punctuation

There are other ways of using context to guess the meaning of unknown words. Sometimes the writer will paraphrase (use other words) to make the meaning clearer to the reader. These paraphrases are often signaled by punctuation. The punctuation which signals paraphrases include:

, (commas)

— (dashes)

( ) (parentheses)

This sentence uses contextual paraphrasing by punctuation:

We sometimes stereotype (label) without realizing it.

In this sentence, the definition of "stereotype" is given in parentheses. It means "label."

➤ READING SKILL PRACTICE: Contextual Paraphrasing by Punctuation

The following sentences use contextual paraphrasing by punctuation. Circle the word being defined. Then underline the definition.

1. I was unable to convince the bike repairman that I honestly wanted to be more in tune, more familiar with my Chinese side, but had never had that opportunity up until now.

2. You see I grew up in the very diverse multi-cultural mix of Hawaii, which is noted for being a melting pot—where cultures are encouraged to blend together.

3. My students still think I am Japanese, and they are incredulous (totally in disbelief) that I write with my left hand.

➤ **TAKING A CLOSER LOOK**

Read "An American Finding Her Chinese Face" again, focusing on details. Circle *a*, *b*, or *c*. Compare your answers with your classmates' answers.

1. The author was surprised that Chinese faces are _____.

    a. so much alike

    b. so ironic

    c. so different

2. The author knew her secret identity would be discovered when she tried to _____.

    a. ride a bike

    b. speak Chinese

    c. repair her bike

3. After spending one year in China, the author felt she could blend in like a native. List details that prove her point.

    She could speak the native language.   _____

    _____   _____

    _____   _____

4. The author returned to China again because she wanted to _____.

    a. feel frustrations

    b. live in two worlds

    c. discover herself

5. The author loves China despite the problems she has with the _____.

    a. students and repair people

    b. food and biking

    c. language and culture

➤ **INTERACTIVE JOURNAL RESPONSE**

Choose one of the following questions and write a response. Be prepared to give an oral summary.

1. The author says that even though she feels at home in the multi-cultural mix of Hawaii, she is still drawn to China and wants to spend time there to discover who she really is. Why do you think she feels this way? Do you think coming to terms with your own cultural identity is important? Why or why not?

2. Do you have a sense of your cultural identity? If not, why not? If you do, what has helped you develop it?

READING TWO

➤ **BEFORE YOU BEGIN**

Work with a partner.

1. Think back to your early teenage years. Do you remember a situation with other people that was difficult for you, or that made you feel embarrassed? Tell your partner what happened.

2. In the following short story, "A Clean Break," the narrator is a teenage boy of Pakistani origin living in the United States. He tells about a difficult experience that he had a few years earlier. Read the first paragraph and the first sentence of the second paragraph. What do you think the story is about?

   a. _____ The boy has a problem because he doesn't like pork.

   b. _____ The boy has a problem because he likes pork.

   c. _____ The boy has a problem because he doesn't eat pork.

➤ **AS YOU READ**

Read the short story "A Clean Break" once, quickly, without your dictionary. Use these questions to help you understand the story as you read.

1. *Who* are the main characters?

2. *Where* does the story take place?

3. *When* does the story take place?

4. *What* happens?

A Clean Break
by Tahira Naqvi

1   Thing is, I don't eat pork, or ham, or for that matter, bacon. We aren't supposed to, you know, because the meat of the pig is *haram*, forbidden. That's one of the first things they tell you in Sunday Islamic class. Then they keep drumming it into your head until the word *pork*, written or uttered, or in any other way implied, instantly conjures up[1] heinous[2] images.

2   Anyway, what I'm saying is that this is something that can lead to problems. Not severe ones, when one thinks of what's going wrong on a larger scale in the world, the ozone layer for example, and the fall of communism, but for a twelve-year-old whose life is confined within the restrictive limits of school and home, matters of ecology or political breakdown of a system thousands of miles away are entirely remote and inconsequential[3]. The pork issue, on the other hand, is immediate, momentous, and disturbing. I can look back now and say all this with a certain degree of complacency because I'm not twelve anymore. My younger brother is. Sooner or later he'll find out the hard way that things are not always what they seem, and as I tell my story I know he must come to grips with[4] this knowledge alone, as I did.

3   It was the summer of '82, or '83 perhaps. We didn't go to Pakistan that year, I got my first A in English, my first D in math, and that was also the year I mowed the lawn[5] for the very first time, taking three days to complete the job. My story unfolds at Dan's house on the occasion of *his* twelfth birthday—Dan, to whom I confided my necessary aversion[6] to pork when we were about eight and who responded by giving me a bite of his ham sandwich saying, with a completely straight face, "Want a bite of my sandwich? It's roast beef." I can't remember now why I was so eager to take a bite from his sandwich in the first place. I'll never forget how he roared and gurgled with laughter afterward.

---

[1] *conjures up:* brings to mind
[2] *heinous:* very evil
[3] *inconsequential:* unimportant
[4] *come to grips with:* learn to deal with
[5] *mowed the lawn:* cut grass with a machine
[6] *aversion:* strong dislike

4   Anyway, Dan's mother, Mrs. Gordon, was serving hot dogs, burgers, and ice cream, regular birthday fare. Now hot dogs are hot dogs. I mean, you can't say no to one or people will tend to view you as weird. Everyone eats hot dogs, even the strictest Muslims who won't eat any kind of meat except that which is *halal* (kosher[7]). So how was I going to put myself in a spot[8] by asking Mrs. Gordon if the hot dogs sizzling with such an air of detachment on the grill were pork or beef?

5   You see, once a hot dog's been stripped and bared of its wrapping, there's no way of telling just by looking at it if it's pork or anything else. Why not wait for the burgers? You might well ask. Well, simply because Mrs. Gordon was doing hot dogs first.

6   We'd been playing freeze tag for nearly an hour and were sweaty and hungry. The hot dogs, ready to perfection, their skins ruddy and streaked with charcoal bands, looked, well, wonderful. My stomach growled audibly. Oh, what agony!

7   I must admit it had never been as bad as this. Ideas about escape presented themselves in an indiscriminate way as I followed Dan and the others in their trek toward food. I could take the hot dog and later toss it behind some bushes when no one was looking; I could take it and hide it under a pile of potato chips, eat the chips slowly, and *then* toss the hot dog behind some bushes; I could take the dreaded[9] thing into the house surreptitiously and dispose of it in the kitchen trash and come out clean; I could politely decline the hot dog saying, "I'm sick, I'm not supposed to eat any meat." The line of kids in front of me diminished. I still didn't know what I was going to do with the hot dog. All I knew was I was going to take it and I wasn't going to eat it.

8   There was much hysteria among us that afternoon. Mustard went flying on shirts and faces instead of being deposited neatly on the hot dogs, ketchup was squirted this way and that, some landing on our T-shirts, some in our hair. Dan was gurgling and roaring again. And on the grill, Mrs. Gordon's long, white, freckled arm poised over it with tongs, the hot dogs continued to hiss[10] maliciously.

---

[7] *kosher*: clean according to Jewish law
[8] *put myself in a spot*: get into an uncomfortable situation
[9] *dreaded*: feared, hated
[10] *hiss*: make a sound like a long, loud S

9   Uncertainty is a terrible thing. And it's never more disturbing than   65
when one is among friends. I wiped my mouth with a paper napkin
and heaped my plate high with chips. Soon the hot dog was buried
under them. Where were the bushes? They were far, oh yes they were
far, at the edge of the lawn, and beyond them was—the road!
Frustration formed a knot in my stomach; I swore silently. There was   70
nothing else to do except sneak into the house and dump the
wretched item.

10   I found myself in the kitchen. There wasn't anyone around. From
the kitchen window I could see the whole gang devouring their hot
dogs. I could also see that Mrs. Gordon had put the hamburger pat-   75
ties on the grill and that they were already smoking. I looked around
for a trash can. None was in sight. Sometimes they're hidden in the
cabinet below the sink—why show the world your trash? I bent
down.

11   "Is that you Hada?"   80

12   Startled, I straightened up quickly to find myself face to face with
Dan's grandmother, who all of us called Mrs. G.

13   "Hi, Mrs. G."

14   "How are you this afternoon? Enjoying your hot dog, I see."

15   If she only knew. "Yeah," I lied. We chatted for a moment longer   85
while she rummaged through a cabinet. What was she looking for?

16   "See you later, Mrs. G.," I said, and made a swift exit through the
kitchen door while her back was turned to me.

17   It would have been foolish to join my friends with the uneaten hot
dog still in my plate. Nobody takes this long to eat one lousy hot   90
dog. Frantically I looked around, wondering what my next move
should be. My hand was numb, the fingers curled around the limp
and soggy paper plate. And I was awfully, dreadfully hungry. My
insides convulsed and my stomach growled fiercely. On the other
side of the lawn, where the woods began, Dan and the others were   95
beginning a game of tag. "Come on," he said, "we're waiting."

18   I decided to return to the kitchen. Perhaps Mrs. G. had found
what she was looking for and was gone. I peered through the kitchen
door. No sign of her. I darted in, deposited the weary hot dog along
with the bent, enfeebled plate on the kitchen counter and turned to   100
leave. Something held me back. I looked around. What was it?

19   Mrs. Gordon's counters were bare and uncluttered, unlike my mother's which had a toaster, toaster oven, food processor, blender, everything out . . . permanently. Where did Dan's mother hide her appliances? Anyway, this is what it was. Sitting on the clean, spotless counter, the plate with the hot dog and a few solitary chips clinging dejectedly[11] to one side of the hot dog stood out as if it were on display. Like an Andy Warhol[12] painting. The napkin was ragged and congealed with a combination of mustard and ketchup.

20   Hastily I swooped up the plate again and made for the trash can that I knew was in the cabinet under the kitchen sink.

21   "Hey man, what's up? You coming?" Dan had come looking for me.

22   "Yeah," I said, letting go of the plate in my hand. It fell soundlessly into the darkness of the trash can. I sighed in relief.

23   Later, after I had consumed, with unnatural urgency, two burgers and more fries, we helped Mrs. Gordon clean up. As we picked up cartons to take back into the house my eyes fell on some hot dogs still intact in their wrappings. Beef, beef, beef, was all I saw.

24   But like I said, once a hot dog has been stripped and bared, there's no way of telling if it's beef or anything else.

---

[11] *dejectedly:* sadly
[12] *Andy Warhol:* an artist who painted careful, detailed pictures of everyday objects

➤ GETTING THE MAIN IDEA

Read the story again more carefully, still without using your dictionary. Check your understanding by filling in this story map. When you finish, discuss your answers with your classmates.

Story Map of "A Clean Break"

1. *Who* is the main character?

   _____

2. *Where* does the story take place?

   a. at a park

   b. at a friend's house

   c. at school

3. *When* does the story take place?

    a. at night

    b. in the afternoon

    c. in the morning

4. *What* is the situation?

    a. What is the occasion? _____

    b. What is the boy served? _____

    c. How does he feel about it? _____

5. Then *what happens*?

    a. What does he try to do first? _____

    b. What does he try to do next? _____

    c. What does he do in the end? _____

6. *How* does the story turn out? What does he discover in the end?

_____

➤ READING SKILL PRACTICE: Vocabulary in Context

Part A: Guessing Meaning from Context

Use the context of the sentence or paragraph to determine the meaning of these words from "A Clean Break." First, find the word in the story by using the paragraph number (in brackets [ ] next to each word). Read the sentence. If the meaning is not clear, keep reading until you can guess the meaning. Then circle the best definition.

1. remote [2]

    a. far away   **b.** too close

2. confided [3]

    a. tell something that's   **b.** offer something to someone
        personal or secret

3. audibly [6]

    a. painfully   **b.** loud enough to hear

4. hysteria [8]

    a. uncontrolled excitement   **b.** uncontrolled sadness

5. devouring [10]

    a. hiding   **b.** eating quickly

6. rummaged [15]

    a. looked for something by moving   **b.** arranged things neatly for display
    things around carelessly

7. enfeebled [18]

    a. very weak   **b.** very strong

8. uncluttered [19]

    a. neat and clean   **b.** messy and dirty

9. congealed [19]

    a. delicious   **b.** thick and sticky

Part B: Contextual Paraphrasing by Punctuation

The author has used contextual paraphrasing to define two words in the short story "A Clean Break." Scan the story to find the sentences that contain contextual paraphrasing. Look for commas, dashes, and parentheses.

1. Circle the word being defined.

2. Underline the definition.

Part C: Guessing Meaning using other Contexts

It is not always possible to guess the meaning of a word from the context of a sentence or paragraph you are reading. Sometimes, however, you can guess the meaning if the word is used again in another context. First, try to guess the meaning of each underlined word in the sentences which appear in the paragraphs of the short story indicated in brackets [ ] below. Then make a second guess based on another context. The first one is done as an example.

1. complacency

    a. I can look back now and say all this with a certain degree of *complacency* because I'm not twelve any more. [2]

    Guess: *complacency* means *being satisfied, not worrying*

    b. The teacher was angry about the student's *complacency* regarding her grades. The teacher planned to tell her that she would fail because her grades were not good enough.

    Guess: *complacency means <u>being satisfied, thinking there is no need to worry when really there is</u>*

2. detachment

    a. So how was I going to put myself in a spot by asking Mrs. Gordon if the hot dogs sizzling with such an air of *detachment* on the grill were pork or beef? [4]

    Guess: *detachment* means _____

    b. After breaking off the relationship with her boyfriend, she could talk about him with an air of *detachment* because she didn't have feelings for him anymore.

    Guess: *detachment* means _____

3. indiscriminate

    a. Ideas about escape presented themselves in an *indiscriminate* way as I followed Dan and the others in their trek toward food. [7]

    Guess: *indiscriminate* means _____

    b. People who watch television a lot are often *indiscriminate* and casual in their choice of programs.

    Guess: *indiscriminate* means _____

4. surreptitiously

    a. I could take the dreaded thing into the house *surreptitiously* and dispose of it in the kitchen trash and come out clean. [7]

    Guess: *surreptitiously* means _____

    b. When no one was looking, the child *surreptitiously* took a puff from the cigarette that was sitting in the ashtray

    Guess: *surreptitiously* means _____

5. maliciously

   a. And on the grill, Mrs. Gordon's long, white, freckled arm poised over it with tongs, the hot dogs continued to hiss *maliciously*. [8]

   Guess: *maliciously* means _____

   b. After they were no longer friends they started to speak *maliciously* about each other, showing how much they now hated each other.

   Guess: *maliciously* means _____

6. wretched

   a. There was nothing else to do except sneak into the house and dump the *wretched* item. [9]

   Guess: *wretched* means _____

   b. They looked *wretched* standing out in the cold rain without a raincoat or even a jacket.

   Guess: *wretched* means _____

Now check your dictionary for the exact meaning of each word. How accurate were your guesses?

➤ **TAKING A CLOSER LOOK**

Discuss these questions with a small group. Choose someone to take notes on your ideas. When you finish, share your ideas with the class.

1. The title, "A Clean Break" is a common phrase in English. It was originally used to describe a fracture or broken bone in which the edges of the break are straight and the bone does not come through the skin. It is painful but not dangerous. "A clean break" is also used when a person takes action to end a difficult situation. For example, someone could make a clean break with a boyfriend or girlfriend when the relationship has become difficult. Think about the action Hada took in the story. What was the "clean break" Hada made?

2. Throughout the story, we can find other words, phrases, and expressions that are commonly used in conversational English. For example, the author

uses expressions such as "anyway," "thing is," and "put myself in a spot." The author uses these expressions to reflect what a teenager like Hada might say when telling his story to someone. Find other examples of this conversational language by skimming the paragraphs listed below. Write down the expressions you find.

Paragraph 1

_____

_____

Paragraph 2

_____

_____

Paragraph 4

_____

_____

Paragraph 5

_____

_____

Paragraph 19

_____

_____

Paragraph 24

_____

_____

3. Hada was uncertain about whether to take the hotdog or refuse it. What fears did Hada have about refusing the hot dog? Do you think his fears were realistic? Why or why not?

4. What points does the author make in this story about cross-cultural situations?

 ➤ COMMUNICATE

Read the situation and prepare a role play for it. Work with a small group.

You are at a party with some of your friends. The host of the party is serving hamburgers and various salads. She offers you a hamburger, not knowing that you are vegetarian.

What do you do in this situation? What do you say? How does your host react? What does she say? What is the reaction of others at the party? How does the situation turn out?

Use the expressions on pages 211-214 of the Appendix to help you.

➤ INTERACTIVE JOURNAL RESPONSE

Choose one of the following questions and write a response. Be prepared to give an oral summary.

1. When they were about eight years old, Dan tricked Hada into eating a ham sandwich by telling him it was roast beef (Paragraph 3). How seriously did Dan take Hada's culture then? Did Dan still feel the same way later, at his twelfth birthday party? Support your answer with evidence from the story.

2. If you were Hada, what would you have done when Dan tricked you into eating ham? Do you think you would have continued to be friends with Dan?

3. Hada feels he doesn't fit in because of the cultural differences that exist between him and his friends. Was there ever a time you felt you didn't fit in? What made you feel that way?

4. Do you feel you have experienced personal growth from a cross-cultural encounter you had? What happened? How did it help you to grow?

CONSUMER LIFESTYLE

We live in a consumer society where quality of life is often defined by what we own. This consumer lifestyle, however, often results in only temporary satisfaction among those who can afford it, and mounting frustration among the many who cannot. Maybe we need to strike a balance between the basic necessities and the luxuries in life to ultimately achieve a good lifestyle.

READING ONE

➤ BEFORE YOU BEGIN

1. What are the reasons for consumerism in your society?

   a. _____ Read the list of ideas below then add two of your own reasons.

   b. _____ Rank these reasons based on your own consumer lifestyle
   (1= most important reason, 4 = least important reason).

   c. _____ When you finish compare your list with a partner.

   _____ as a basic need _____

   _____ as a way to express yourself _____

   _____ _____

   _____ _____

Companies selling brand name clothes and products are using creative forms of
advertising to appeal to consumers all over the world. Does such advertising
influence you? Why or why not?

➤ AS YOU READ

Skim "Consumer Lifestyle" to get an idea of what the article is about.

CONSUMER LIFESTYLE
by Elisabeth Malkin, from *Business Week*

1   It's Friday night, and 24-year-old Javier Vega is hanging out with
his friends in Condesa, a Mexico City neighborhood that has become
a hangout[1] for the young and hip. Before nightfall, rich kids descend
from the hills in new cars and strut along the street while talking on
their cell phones. Students linger over coffee at outdoor cafes.   5
Dressed head-to-toe in the latest imported gear, Vega—a law student
who moonlights[2] as a fashion designer— surveys the scene. "Brands
have a certain personality," he says. "I want a certain personality
and a certain lifestyle, so I go for those brands."

---

[1] *hangout:* a place where people spend time together
[2] *moonlights:* has a second job, sometimes at night

2   Vega and his friends are the reason marketers flock to youth   10
hangouts like Condesa these days. Companies are battling as never
before for the hearts, minds, and wallets of Mexico's biggest consumer
segment: the 25-and-under set. "They're the critical target for
both today's and tomorrow's sales," says Joanne Black, director of
marketing for Jugos del Valle, a Mexican juicemaker. That's a reality   15
marketers in Mexico are increasingly waking up to, as demographic
trends[3] push the number of young consumers higher every year.
And unlike their parents, this generation has no qualms about
consumerism. It's their new lifestyle.

3   Most of these kids, however, don't have much money to spend.   20
Some two-thirds of Mexican teens and twentysomethings are poor
or working class. But what this market lacks in cash it more than
makes up for in size. Some 23 million Mexicans, or 23% of the
population, are between the ages of 14 and 24. And the money they
drop[4] on such small-ticket items as colas, snacks, and CDs can add   25
up to big figures. Antenna Consulting, a Mexico City research firm,
estimates that spending by Mexicans aged 13 to 18 comes to $10
billion a year.

4   Still marketers are having to work harder than ever before to grab
the attention of these kids. Thanks to trade liberalization and foreign   30
investment, Mexico's young people are now exposed to a broad
array of brands, from candy to cars. "This is the first generation in
Mexico that's a generation of choice," says Liz Paul, president of
marketing services for Antenna. "This is also a generation that has been
blitzed[5] with advertising from an early age. That means companies   35
must come up with creative ways to win them over. Their response
to advertisers—'surprise me or don't invade my space.'"

5   Advertisers can't just look north of the border[6] for inspiration,
though. Teenage rebellion, a popular theme in the US, just doesn't go
down well in Mexico. Unlike US kids, one-half to two-thirds of   40
Mexicans ages 14 to 24 get all their spending money from their parents,
according to a study by Antenna. "You can see somebody on the
street with tattoos, earrings and purple hair, but he's still with

---

[3] *demographic trends:* a general movement in population statistics, eg., increase in
    births, decrease in deaths, etc.
[4] *money they drop:* money they spend
[5] *blitzed:* attacked
[6] *north of the border:* at the United States

Mommy and Daddy," says Carmen Arce, MTV Latin America's Mexico veejay[7]. She should know: at 24, Arce still lives with her parents, as do almost three-quarters of Mexicans aged 21 to 24. Other things US youth have embraced that have not caught on in Mexico include mountain biking and natural foods. Young Mexicans "are global brand consumers, but they're not global trend followers," says Antenna's Paul.

6   For marketers courting Mexico's increasingly sophisticated teens and twentysomethings, it's also no longer enough to run ads on top-rated TV shows and radio stations that appeal to older adults as well. So some consumer-product companies are turning to outlets that narrowly target the market segment they desire.

7   One of these is MTV Latin America. In Mexico, where cable TV reaches only 15% of households, MTV was once dismissed as a channel for a tiny Americanized elite. Not now, says Juan I. Ruiz de Ojeda, a brand manager at Coca-Cola Mexico. Ojeda commissioned a survey of teens in out-of-the-way places in Mexico last year and learned that 70% to 80% of them were familiar with MTV. They watched it at friends' houses or on pirated[8] cable hookups. Based on that research, the company launched a promotion for Sprite on the music video channel in September. In a follow-up poll, the percentage of respondents who agreed that Sprite is a brand that "really understands young people" jumped almost 20 points.

8   For the same reasons, marketers are also going online. Although Internet penetration is only about 4% at present, users are overwhelmingly young. New York-based StarMedia Networks Inc., a Spanish- and Portuguese-language portal, claims that 78% of its users are under 35. Moreover, thanks to the increase of special-interest chat rooms and sites, companies can now target the narrowest of segments. These days, Mexican kids can have a lifestyle their parents could only dream about. They are waking up to consumerism, and how.

---

[7] *veejay:* a person who plays music videos on TV
[8] *pirated:* used illegally

➤ GETTING THE MAIN IDEA

The author's main idea is:

a. ⎯⎯⎯ Mexican kids are becoming stylish global brand consumers.

b. ⎯⎯⎯ The attitudes of Mexican kids these days are similar to those of their parents.

c. ⎯⎯⎯ Mexican advertising companies are having difficulty reaching Mexican kids.

➤ VOCABULARY IN CONTEXT

These sentences contain vocabulary from the reading "Consumer Lifestyle." Circle the best definition for the underlined world.

1. They like to <u>linger</u> over dinner, talking, eating, and enjoying the time together.

    a. spend a long time

    b. hurry

    c. make a decision

2. I have no <u>qualms</u> about the course because I enjoy the classes and know I can do well.

    a. doubts

    b. interest

    c. information

3. Talking with the artist gave me great <u>inspiration</u> for my own work.

    a. money

    b. problems

    c. new ideas

4. He <u>was exposed to</u> music at a very young age because his parents were musicians.

    a. experienced

    b. was unaware of

    c. was surprised by

5. She <u>embraced</u> the idea and began to tell others about it too.

   a. disagreed with

   b. wasn't sure about

   c. agreed with

►READING SKILL: Scanning for Details

Students are often asked to find specific details such as facts, dates, names, and other important information about a reading passage. Good readers scan—they move their eyes quickly down the page in search of the information they are looking for. Through scanning practice you will become a faster and more focused reader.

►READING SKILL PRACTICE: Scanning for Details

Scan the reading and choose the best answers.

1. Kids in Mexico choose designer brands because they _____.

   a. want good quality

   b. want a certain lifestyle

   c. are trend followers

2. Marketers of designer brands want to attract _____.

   a. the 25-and-under segment of Mexican society

   b. adults who listen to TV and radio

   c. parents who pay for the designer brands their kids want

3. Mexican teenagers spend a total of around _____ a year on small items.

   a. $23 million

   b. $10 million

   c. $18 million

4. Teenagers in Mexico have more choice than their parents had thanks to _____.

    a. advertising

    b. government policies

    c. consumer pressure

5. Advertising in Mexico has to be _____ to attract young Mexican consumers.

    a. the same as in the US

    b. creative

    c. with music videos

6. The reading says that _____.

    a. US teenagers get most of their spending money from their parents

    b. rebellion is a popular theme for advertisers in the US

    c. tattoos, earrings, and purple hair are signs of rebellion in Mexico

7. The music video channel MTV is _____.

    a. not popular with Mexican teenagers

    b. only popular with rich Mexican teenagers who follow US trends

    c. an attractive source of advertising for consumer-market companies

8. One reason marketers are going online is because _____.

    a. they can target young people in Mexico

    b. they can advertise in both Spanish and Portuguese

    c. they can target only rich Mexicans

► TAKING A CLOSER LOOK

Read "Consumer Lifestyle" again, focusing on details. Are these sentences true (**T**) or false (**F**)? Underline a sentence or phrase in the reading that supports your answer. When you finish, compare your answers with your classmates' answers.

1. _____ Condesa is a restaurant in downtown Mexico City.

2. _____ Most Mexican kids have a lot of money to spend these days.

3. _____ There are few foreign goods in Mexico because of government regulations.

4. _____ Companies in Mexico depend on creative advertising to sell their products.

5. _____ Mexican teenagers do not depend on their parents for money.

6. _____ Mexican teenagers follow the same trends as US teenagers do.

7. _____ The music channel MTV has a definite influence on young Mexican consumers.

8. _____ Most Mexicans using the Internet are over the age of 35.

➤ INTERACTIVE JOURNAL RESPONSE

Choose one of these questions and write a response. Be prepared to give an oral summary.

1. According to this article, young people in Mexico are embracing consumerism, something their parents could only dream about. How might this new lifestyle benefit Mexican society? How might it harm Mexican society?

2. What effects has consumerism had on your society, on your environment?

3. Are you satisfied with your lifestyle? Why or why not?

READING TWO

➤ BEFORE YOU BEGIN

1. What is the meaning of frugal? Check your dictionary if you are not sure.

2. Do you think most people in your country live a frugal lifestyle? Do you live frugally?

3. Why might someone lead a frugal life?

4. Based on the title of this reading, "A Frugal Alternative?," do you think the author will:

   a. encourage the idea of a frugal lifestyle

   b. discourage the idea of a frugal lifestyle

   c. examine the idea of a frugal lifestyle

➤ AS YOU READ

Skim "A Frugal Alternative?" to get an idea of what the article is about.

A FRUGAL ALTERNATIVE?
by James Griffin, from *The UNESCO Courier*

1   Can frugality lead to a better quality of life? Or is it just another lifestyle—admirable[1] in its way, perhaps, but no more admirable than a consumer lifestyle can be? Is frugality any more firmly rooted in values than consumerism? Or is it, perhaps, valuable only in special circumstances, when food or clothes or other goods are in short supply and sparing consumption is only good sense? Is it a virtue[2] in the Third World but not in the First? Is it appropriate in some settings and inappropriate in others? Of what value is a frugal lifestyle?

2   Well, let's first imagine what a frugal life is: I am sparing in all that I use; I consume enough for health but no more than required to meet simple, basic needs. Now imagine a non-frugal life: I am less careful about what and how much I use; I consume more than is strictly needed for my basic needs. Now if someone sees these two lives apart from any consequences they might have, is there any reason to say that one is better than the other? I see no reason to think so.

3   So if a frugal life is in some way valuable, it must be because of the things it leads to. In other words, frugality must offer benefits, not simply privation[3]. And here, it seems to me, there is an interesting case.

_____

[1] *admirable:* very good
[2] *virtue:* good quality
[3] *privation:* not having the things you need in life

4   Frugality strikes most modern people as out of date[4]. It seems   30
appropriate and necessary when there is not enough to go around or
when people are poor, but as the world grows richer, frugality grows
irrelevant. A human today is seen as a complex of desires. The quality
of a human life is seen as in direct proportion to the satisfaction of
these desires. But one cannot equate what makes a person's life good   35
with what satisfies that person's desires. It is possible—in fact, all too
common—for a person's desires to be satisfied and the person be no
better off or happier about his or her life.

5   Nothing becomes valuable just by being desired. Some things in
life are valuable and others not. That is a strong claim, but it seems   40
right. I think that, with experience, we can compile a list of the
valuable things in life—the things that may not make every life
better (people are too various for that) but that may make most
normal human lives better. My list would contain at least these
unsurprising things: enjoyment, deep personal relations, accomplishing   45
something in the course of one's life, understanding certain basic
moral matters, autonomy[5], and liberty.

6   One all too common feature of the life of a modern consumer is
that one set of desires is satisfied only to be succeeded by a new set,
with no advance in quality of life. When that happens, it is clear that   50
one has lost sight of values. What are really valuable are the things
on the list that I just mentioned.

7   This, it seems to me, is where frugality comes in. Frugality is
valuable if, and only if a frugal style of life is generally conducive[6]
to some of the values on the list. For example, a frugal lifestyle   55
tends to be a simple life, and, though simplicity in life is not guaranteed
to put one in touch with real values, it increases the chances that
one will be. Many of us from time to time have had the experience
of living more simply than we usually do and finding ourselves, as
a result, more in harmony with what matters in life. Of course, we   60
return to our everyday life and lose this precious insight[7], but at
least we have had that experience. Frugality can, in this instrumental
way, be a personal good.

---

[4] *out of date:* not fashionable anymore
[5] *autonomy:* independence, being able to run one's own life
[6] *conducive:* contributes, helps to bring about something good
[7] *insight:* deep understanding

8   It can also be a community good. A frugal community can save and invest for a better future. Frugality can also be a global good—indeed,   65 a little more frugality may be necessary simply to avoid global disaster. Our consumerism pollutes the atmosphere, producing global warming. We certainly do not know all the consequences in store for us from that.

9   But I must not end with praise of frugality. My life is better because I choose to live simply on holidays, consuming much less than I   70 normally do. But then I live in the prosperous[8] part of the world. I am able choose simplicity. It would feel very different if I were *forced* to consume sparingly. I do not think my life would be better for it.

_____

[8] *prosperous:* rich

➤ GETTING THE MAIN IDEA

The author's main idea is:

a. _____ We all need to consume less in order to improve the environment.

b. _____ We need to think about how we live our life.

c. _____ We should never worry about how we live our life.

➤ VOCABULARY IN CONTEXT

These sentences contain vocabulary from the reading "A Frugal Alternative?" Read each sentence and circle the best definition for the underlined world.

1. You do not have to take the English writing course; it is <u>optional</u>.

    a. a choice

    b. required

    c. helpful

2. She was <u>sparing</u> with her use of heat and light; she didn't want to use too much energy.

    a. exact

    b. careful

    c. careless

3. This textbook is <u>appropriate</u> for your level of English.

    a. unnecessary

    b. right

    c. wrong

4. Athletes <u>consume</u> large amounts of food while training.

    a. use up

    b. like

    c. take out

5. Please be <u>vigilant</u> when marking the exams; we do not want to make mistakes.

    a. powerful

    b. easy

    c. careful

6. The details he told us were <u>irrelevant</u>; we needed to look for new information.

    a. untrue

    b. unrelated

    c. satisfactory

➤ READING SKILL: Scanning for Details

Scanning for details improves comprehension. It helps you identify the main details of a reading and *selectively* forces you to process the information you read.

➤ READING SKILL PRACTICE: Scanning for Details

Scan the passage quickly to find answers to these questions. Then, in your own words, write complete sentences to answer each one.

1. According to the author, what is the main difference between a frugal life and a non-frugal life?

    _____

    _____

2. According to the author, when might a frugal lifestyle be appropriate?

_____

_____

3. Why might modern people not value a frugal lifestyle?

_____

_____

4. How is the quality of human life measured these days?

_____

_____

5. What are six valuable things in life according to the author?

_____

_____

6. According to the author how can frugality bring about: a) personal good, b) community good, c) global good?

_____

_____

➤ TAKING A CLOSER LOOK

Read "A Frugal Alternative" again, this time focusing on more details. Decide if these sentences are true (**T**) or false (**F**). Underline a sentence or phrase that supports your answer. When you finish, compare your answers with your classmates' answers.

1. _____ The author thinks a frugal lifestyle is only desirable in the Third World.

2. _____ The author believes living a frugal life is best.

3. _____ According to the author, a frugal lifestyle would not seem fashionable to modern people.

4. _____ The author claims that once we get what we want, we'll be satisfied.

5. _____ The author states that by acquiring what we desire our quality of life will improve.

6. _____ The author thinks that if we can experience the things we value, it is worthwhile to lead a frugal life.

➤ COMMUNICATE

Most people agree that it is important to have a good quality of life. However, defining "quality of life" is difficult, and not everyone defines it in the same way. Most people do agree, however, that it means more than just having material things in life. What are the factors that constitute a good quality of life for you?

1. Make a list of 5 factors you think constitute a good quality of life. State the reasons for each of your choices. (Refer back to the reading for ideas.)

2. When you finish, get together with a partner and compare your lists. Be prepared to explain the reasons for your choices.

My Quality of Life Factors	
Factor	**Reason Chosen**
1.	
2.	
3.	
4.	
5.	

Use the expressions for Giving Reasons on page 212 to help you.

➤ INTERACTIVE JOURNAL RESPONSE

Choose one of these questions and write a response. Be prepared to give an oral summary.

1. The author claims his life is better because he lives simply on holidays, consuming much less than normal (paragraph 9). What could you do in order to consume less and live more simply? Would it make your life better? Why or why not?

2. According to the author, consumerism pollutes the atmosphere, producing global warming (paragraph 8). What forms of consumerism pose the greatest threat to the health of the planet? What steps can people take to reduce this threat? Use the Internet and library resources to research this topic.

3. If you were advising someone on how to live their life would you recommend frugality? Explain.

AGING

Most of us want to live a long life. But in fact, growing old can bring problems: loneliness, poor health, poverty. As nuclear families replace extended families, we often lose touch with our elderly family members. Old people hold a key to the past: their long experience and wisdom can enrich younger lives. Addressing the issues of aging is essential for a stable and emotionally rich society.

READING ONE

➤ BEFORE YOU BEGIN

Look at the graph and fill in the summary below it.

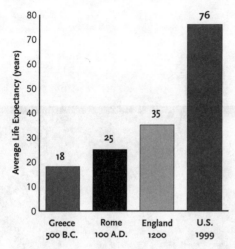

Source: Adapted from The Sociology of Aging by Diana Harris and William Cole, Houghton Mifflin, 1980, and the United Nations Statistics Division, 1999.

People are living _____ than before. For example, about _____
                        (1)   (2)
years ago, people in _____ did not expect to live past 35 years, but
                          (3)
today, they live to be _____ years old.
                             (4)

Discuss these questions with a partner:

1. How long would you like to live? Why?

2. Do you know any people who are over the age of 80, and still healthy? What is their secret to a long healthy life? In your opinion, what is the key to staying healthy and alert in old age?

➤ AS YOU READ

Skim "How to Grow Old and Stay Young" to get an idea of what the article is about.

How to Grow Old and Stay Young
by Michael Brickey, from *The Futurist*

1   The oldest known human is documented in the Guinness Book of World Records as Jeanne Calment from Arles, France, who lived to be 122 years old. When asked her secret to long life, Jeanne answered, "I took pleasure where I could. I acted clearly and morally and without regret. And I'm very lucky." In the years ahead, more people will be living decades longer than their parents did. In the last century, American life expectancy increased some 64%, from about 47 years to 76. The US Census Bureau predicts that in 2050 we will have one million centenarians as the leading edge of the Baby Boom generation starts turning 100. There is a dramatic contrast between those who age well and those who don't. What distinguishes people who are still mentally and physically sharp at age 100? Of course, one secret to health in old age is simply in the genes: Calment's mother was alert and healthy at 86, her father, similarly youthful at 93. Another well-known factor is exercise: recent research into the field of "neurogenesis" (the production of new nerve cells) suggests that new brain cells are formed during vigorous exercise. But new research indicates that an important factor in staying youthful in old age is a particular set of mental attitudes.

2   The first powerful mental outlook is optimism, the tendency to expect that results will be good. Optimism has been the subject of a multitude of research studies. The findings are clear: optimists are healthier, happier and more successful, and they live longer and recover from illnesses better. One important aspect of optimism is the way optimists think about the causes of events. They tend to believe that a good event is the result of their own skill or effort, but that a bad event is the result of chance. This gives them hope to keep on trying. On the other hand, pessimists have a negative bias in their interpretation and believe that if they have a good result, it's not connected to their own skill or effort. In other words, they think success is not under their control. Yet, strangely, in the case of a negative event, pessimists tend to blame themselves for failure, believing that it was their lack of skill or effort that brought about the bad result.

3   Optimists can use their positive mind set to weather life's discouragements. But when pessimists become ill or face hard times, they

often give up or become depressed. They tend to believe there is
nothing they can do; consequently, they do less than optimists do to
help themselves. Since they may be less likable than optimists, they
also tend to have fewer friends—another factor that contributes to
higher risk for illness and slower recovery from illness.   40

4   The second key to eternal youth is gratitude. Gratitude is connected
to perspective, that is, judging the importance or non-importance of
events. Maintaining a sense of perspective can help us stay calm
when life's problems could trigger an angry, unhealthy response. For
example, some people go into road rage[1] when stuck in traffic or   45
bothered by another driver. They let themselves become very upset
over small inconveniences and minor insults. When delayed by traffic,
try remembering how comfortable your air-conditioned or heated car
is, with its collection of your favorite CDs. That is, focus on the
positive aspects of your situation, even if it is frustrating or incon-   50
venient. Perspective includes the realization that one setback does
not ruin your life. Often a difficult time has an upside to it.
Basketball great Michael Jordan was cut from his high school varsity
basketball team his sophomore year because he wasn't giving it his
all. Jordan said, "It was the best thing that ever happened to me."   55
Planning on living to 120 makes it easier to gain perspective: it's hard
to believe that one setback is going to ruin the next hundred years
of your life. And by focusing on the positive aspects of even a bad
situation, you will feel gratitude and happiness.

5   The third mental attitude is to be "proactive," that is, to deal with   60
problems as soon as or even before they appear rather than letting
them develop into crises. Many people have difficulty dealing with
problems. They ruminate[2] constantly, they are inflexible, and they
procrastinate[3]. Centenarians rarely have these traits. Procrastinators
focus on how they feel about doing something instead of the outcome   65
they desire. When he tries to do his homework, the procrastinator
envisions himself struggling with the difficult reading or questions,
and feeling bored or frustrated. He then imagines an alternative, a
television program, and asks himself how that feels. It feels good, so
he turns on the television. People who overcome procrastination are   70

---

[1] *road rage:* aggressive behavior resulting from the frustration of driving
[2] *ruminate:* to think something over for a long time
[3] *procrastinate:* to delay doing something

able to "just get it done" by thinking about the finished product and imagining the eventual satisfaction and rewards. Many centenarians possess an internal voice that says "Just do it."

6   Dealing with problems involves taking care of interpersonal conflicts. Most centenarians have learned to get rid of their "baggage"—those old conflicts with parents, siblings, friends, partners, and children. Our minds and bodies use a lot of energy to hold on to anger and resentments, which distracts us from more important matters. Centenarians have learned that "dealing with it" means forgiving, letting go of past issues, and focusing on the positive and what is happening now.

7   Finally, the last key to a healthy, happy, old age is to embrace learning and change.

8   In Cuba and the United States in the early part of the twentieth century, thousands of bored workers rolled cigars. To help relieve the tedium of this work, the cigar companies hired professional readers with great voices to read literature and newspapers to the workers on the job. For four hours a day, the workers were treated to a classical education; they might not have gone to high school, but they were lifelong learners. Today's equivalent would be people who listen to informative programs on public radio. Indeed, the libraries and the Internet have democratized[4] access to information. As a result, we can be lifelong learners without even leaving our homes. Technological and social changes are happening more quickly today. If you want to live a long and healthy life, you must be able to learn new things and cope with change. You need to maintain enough ties with your past to give you a sense of security, while embracing enough new information and change to make life interesting.

9   You are never too old or too young to seek and follow good role models. Centenarians who are sharp mentally and physically show us that these four attitudes are a foundation for good health, long life, and happiness.

---

[4] *democratize:* to make something available to everyone

➤ READING SKILL: Main Idea

Identifying the topic of a reading is the first step in understanding the main idea. In Unit 1, you learned to pick up the topic of the article by noticing the title and skimming the first and last sentences of the article.

Which best identifies the topic of the reading?

    a. _____ the benefits of exercise

    b. _____ staying youthful in old age

    c. _____ aging and its problems

To grasp the main idea, you need to read more carefully to understand what the author wants to say about the topic. In this case, the topic is "how to stay youthful in old age." To understand the main idea of the passage, we ask ourselves, "What does the author want to tell me about staying youthful in old age?" You can often find the main idea in the last sentence of the introduction (first paragraph). The main idea is then developed in different ways in each body paragraph, with examples and supporting details. Finally, in the conclusion (last paragraph), the main idea is usually summarized or repeated.

➤ READING SKILL PRACTICE: Main Idea

Follow these steps to identify the main idea:

1. Read the introduction again, carefully. Notice the last sentence of the introduction (which you have already underlined in *As You Read*).

2. Choose the best summary statement of the main idea as it is expressed in the last sentence of the introduction:

    a. _____ We need to accept the fact of growing old and eventually dying, rather than struggle against it.

    b. _____ People are too worried about looking young even when they are 100 years old.

    c. _____ Staying healthy in old age requires certain mental attitudes.

3. Now read the rest of the passage, noticing how the main idea from the introduction is developed and supported by examples. Notice the first sentence of each body paragraph (which you have already underlined in *As You Read*). Then, in your own words, summarize the main idea as it is expressed in the conclusion:

_____

_____

➤ GETTING THE MAIN IDEA

Check your answer to number 3 above. Choose the best summary of the main idea as it is expressed in the conclusion:

1. _____ Staying healthy in old age requires four attitudes: optimism, gratitude, proactive problem solving, and embracing learning and change.

2. _____ The most important way to stay healthy in old age is be thankful for what life brings you.

3. _____ Being able to cope with change is the key factor in staying healthy in old age.

➤ VOCABULARY IN CONTEXT

These sentences contain vocabulary from "How to Grow Old and Stay Young." Read each sentence and circle the best definition for the underlined word.

1. He spent one hour <u>asserting</u> that he was innocent, but the police still arrested him.

   a. saying that something is true

   b. denying that something is true

   c. forgetting what really happened

2. Nobody likes him because he tends to <u>discount</u> other people's achievements.

   a. ignore

   b. praise

   c. talk about

3. The boy would often <u>amplify</u> the importance of gifts, saying that he would die if he didn't receive a new bicycle or a new baseball bat.

    a. reduce

    b. increase

    c. complain about

4. That tough soldier has learned <u>to weather</u> miserable conditions.

    a. become ill

    b. live safely through

    c. complain about

5. The small child's noisy behavior tended <u>to trigger</u> his mother's anger.

    a. to calm down

    b. to solve

    c. to cause

6. If someone <u>envisions</u> winning a million dollars, they usually smile.

    a. imagines

    b. refuses

    c. misses

7. My cat often <u>distracts me</u> from my work.

    a. helps me with

    b. teaches me about

    c. takes my attention away

8. The <u>tedium</u> of the class made the students fall asleep.

    a. excitement

    b. discomfort

    c. boredom

➤ TAKING A CLOSER LOOK

Read "How to Grow Old and Stay Young" again, focusing on details. Are these sentences true (**T**) or false (**F**)? Underline a sentence or phrase in the reading that supports your answer. When you finish, compare your answers with your classmates' answers.

1. _____ By 2050 there will be one thousand centenarians in the US.

2. _____ Genetics and exercise play an important role in a healthy long life.

3. _____ Optimists have more health problems than pessimists.

4. _____ Pessimists and optimists interpret the causes of events in different ways.

5. _____ Optimists don't try as hard as pessimists to help themselves.

6. _____ By *gratitude* the author means *focusing on the positive aspects of life*.

7. _____ Centenarians are often procrastinators.

8. _____ Procrastinators focus on how they feel about doing something.

9. _____ Being proactive can include forgiving a friend or family member.

10. _____ Accepting change is important for a healthy long life.

➤ INTERACTIVE JOURNAL RESPONSE

Choose one of these questions and write a response. Be prepared to give an oral summary.

1. Interview an elderly person in your family or neighborhood. Ask them these questions:

   • When did you start working?

   • What kind of work did you do?

   • What was the happiest year of your life?

   • In your opinion, what is the secret to a long, healthy, happy life?

   • What do you like best about your life these days?

- What worries you the most about the future?

- What do you think is the most important problem of today's society?

From your interview notes, write a summary of your interviewee's comments.

2. Of the four attitudes mentioned in this reading, which one do you think is the most important in creating health and happiness? Why do you think so?

3. Of the four attitudes mentioned in this reading, is there one which you find particularly difficult to follow in your own life? Explain.

4. Describe your personal experience with elderly people. Has there been one elderly person who has been especially important in your life (for example, a grandparent, a neighbor)? Does (did) he or she have the four mental attitudes mentioned in "How to Grow Old and Stay Young?"

READING TWO

➤ BEFORE YOU BEGIN

Think about these questions:

1. Have you ever lost your keys? When, where, and what happened? How did you feel?

2. In this story an old man loses his keys. Imagine: Which keys? How? What does he do? How does he feel?

3. What other things do old people lose? (consider physical or emotional losses).

Share your ideas with a partner.

➤ AS YOU READ

Read the short story, "Lost Keys," once, quickly, without your dictionary. Use these questions to guide your reading:

- Who are the main characters?

- Where does the story take place?

- When does the story take place?

- What happens?

LOST KEYS
by Paul Milenski

1   The old *dziadz*[1] was always the first out of the car, heading downstream, fishing as rapidly as the flow of water until he put some distance between him and me. I used to kid[2] him about it in the company of my brother when all three of us went ice fishing together, standing out on early ice, three figures suspended above   5 water like crystal, waiting for red-flagged signals on our tips[3]. "Maybe that's why you never took to trout fishing, Ron. The old *dziadz* does not like to keep company. Isn't that right, dziadz?"

2   "Together, you just scare fish on a stream. You need distance. You know that."   10

3   "Ron's sociable, that's why he likes it on the ice."

4   "He's right, dziadz. When I went with you, I felt like a horse left at the gate[4]."

5   "Either you fish right or you don't."

6   The old *dziadz* drove, had his boots on, his pole put together, the   15 crawlers[5] in a shirt pocket. After he parked the car near the stream, he tossed you the keys and he was gone. "I'll catch you later."

7   Then, in an hour or two, he would appear quietly, instantaneously, like a stag[6] poking its head through the brush, taking you by surprise. "How are you doing?"   20

8   After his retirement, he slowed down a little. Once he fell on a slippery rock, broke his glasses. Another time, he got caught in the middle of the stream in a swirling current[7], filled his boots, had to carry half the stream with him to make it to shore. Then, he turned his ankle terrible when he dropped himself from a high bank to the stream bed.   25

9   He began to keep the keys. I asked why, and he said, "So you won't have to worry about them."

10   The last time out it rained. A cold rain, hard and steady. I caught lots of browns[8], orange-bellied, hook-jawed. They were right in the

---

[1] *dziadz:* a Polish word which means "grandfather"
[2] *to kid:* to joke with, to tease
[3] *red-flagged signals on our tips:* little red flags on the fishing lines that move when a fish bites
[4] *like a horse left at the gate:* a race horse that didn't start with the other horses
[5] *crawlers:* night crawlers, big worms caught at night to use for fishing bait
[6] *stag:* an adult male deer
[7] *current:* water moving in a certain direction
[8] *browns:* brown trout (fish)

middle of the stream, in the rain-swollen currents. You had to get in   30
there, fight the swiftness of the water.

11   We did not meet on the stream as usual. When I returned to the
car, he was already there. He was sitting on the wet ground, his back
up against a wheel hub. His clothes were soaked, his hair matted
down, his curl gone. His lips were blue.   35

12   "Did you limit out[9] already?"

13   I am sure he heard me.

14   "Did you quit early?"

15   His voice was barely audible. "I lost the car keys."

16   He was somewhere on the stream, so he said, reaching into his   40
pockets for a handkerchief to wipe dirt from his eyes because he was
whipped by a streamside branch. That's when he realized he did not
have the keys.

17   "Maybe you locked them in the car?"

18   He said he had already checked, through the foggy windows, the   45
ignition, the car seat, the mat. He had traced his path along the
stream, back and forth. No keys.

19   "I swear I'm losing everything lately."

20   "One set of keys—that happens."

21   "Now what are we going to do?" He made a face that I'd never   50
seen him make before; there was so much pain in it. His lips were
twisted, his eyes almost pressed closed by the compression of his
skin.

22   I suggested we walk to the nearest house, call my brother, ask him
to deliver a spare set of keys. He did not like this idea. I said we   55
could hide our equipment under the car or in the brush, bum a
ride[10], be driven back later. This was no good. I asked if he wanted
to look some more; maybe two of us working together would spot
them. No, his looking had been enough.

23   What was left?   60

24   "I deserve to be left out here in the rain."

25   "What kind of talk is that?"

26   "I'm losing everything lately."

27   "I'm not listening to that."

28   "It's true."   65

---

[9] *to limit out:* to have caught all the fish you are allowed by law to catch in one day
[10] *to bum a ride:* to get a ride in someone's car (friend or stranger)

29   "No, it's not. Jesus, one set of car keys."

30   "I don't even remember taking them out of the ignition. That's the real truth of it."

31   "Check your pockets again."

32   "I did."   70

33   "Inside your boot. Maybe they fell in there, are hooked over the leg strap."

34   "I'd feel them there, wouldn't I? Wouldn't I feel them there, rubbing against my leg?"

35   "Maybe not."   75

36   "I would hear them jingle[11], I think. Wouldn't I hear them when I walked?"

37   Then, unaccountably, he moved back down to the stream, staring blankly into the water.

38   I noticed the keys. They were lying near the wheel hub, where he   80
had sat on them, in the indentation from the weight of his body.

39   I called to him, told him when he came back that he had given them to me, and I had forgotten. But I saw clearly that this did not work. He dropped his head as though it were a burden, spent a lot of time on this our last trip together standing in the rain, continuing   85
to look at the ground, not wanting to be the first to take his pole apart, not wanting to leave.

_____

[11] *to jingle:* to make a sound like bells

➤ VOCABULARY IN CONTEXT

These sentences contain vocabulary from the story "Lost Keys." Read each sentence and circle the best definition for the underlined word.

  1. The mouse disappeared <u>instantaneously</u> when we turned on the light, so we could not catch it.

     a. slowly

     b. suddenly

     c. angrily

2. Be careful! The ice on the sidewalk is <u>slippery</u>.

   a. safe

   b. easy to walk on

   c. easy to slide and fall on

3. The <u>swiftness</u> of the water made it difficult to walk across the river.

   a. slowness

   b. pollution

   c. speed

4. Could you speak more loudly? Your voice is not <u>audible</u>.

   a. loud enough to hear

   b. strange

   c. beautiful

5. I can't explain his behavior. He is acting <u>unaccountably</u>.

   a. wisely

   b. without an obvious reason

   c. with an obvious reason

6. You look tired. Put down your <u>burden</u> and take a rest.

   a. heavy weight

   b. light weight

   c. anger

➤ TAKING A CLOSER LOOK

Part A: Dialogue

To make sure you understand the dialogue (the parts in quotation marks: " . . . "), go back and read those parts carefully. Label the dialogue by writing *N* for narrator or *G* for grandfather beside each sentence in quotation marks. One sentence is said by the narrator's brother Ron (*R*).

Part B: Character Analysis

Look at these phrases which describe the old man's behavior before he retires:

"always the first out of the car"

"fishing as rapidly as the flow of water"

"the old dziadz does not like to keep company"

"after he parked the car, he tossed you the keys"

What kind of personality does he seem to have? List three adjectives:

_____   _____   _____

After his retirement, the old man's behavior changes. What are some examples of his changed behavior?

_____

_____

_____

_____

Part C: Character and Motivation

It is interesting to imagine the characters' motivation for their actions. In your opinion, why do the characters do these things?

Action	Motivation
- before retirement, the old man didn't keep the car keys	
- after retirement, the old man begins to keep the keys	
- the grandson lies to his grandfather: he says that he forgot that the old man gave him the keys	
- the old man is reluctant to take apart his fishing pole and doesn't want to leave	

➤ **READING SKILL: Literary Theme as Main Idea**

A newspaper article or textbook essay usually has one main idea which is stated clearly in the introduction and/or conclusion. However, pieces of literature (fiction, drama, poetry) usually have many levels of meaning that are suggested by the author, and the reader has some freedom in interpreting the meaning. There is usually a topic which is based on the facts of the story (the "plot"), and a literary theme (main idea) which expresses a psychological truth about society and human nature. Unlike in prose, this topic, plot, and theme are not expressed in one sentence by the author. The reader has to arrive at the theme by reading and responding to the whole story.

➤ **READING SKILL PRACTICE: Literary Theme as Main Idea**

Try these questions about the main ideas of "Lost Keys":

1. What is the main topic of this story?

   a. _____ aging

   b. _____ ice fishing

   c. _____ keys

2. Which is the best summary of the plot?

   a. _____ This is a story about a grandfather's last fishing trip.

   b. _____ This is a story about a stubborn old man who is hard to get along with.

   c. _____ This is a story about fishing in America.

3. Stating the literary theme (main idea) is up to the reader. What universal truth(s) do you think the author wants to show us about aging, about grandfather-grandson relationships, about family conflict, etc.?

   _____

   _____

   _____

► COMMUNICATE

1. Write another ending for this story (4–5 sentences).

2. Share your idea with a partner.

3. Together, decide on the most interesting ending and create a dialogue between the grandfather and grandson which will change the ending of the story. Be ready to perform it for the class.

Use the expressions for Responding to Ideas on page 112 of the Appendix to help you.

► INTERACTIVE JOURNAL RESPONSE

Choose one of these questions and write a response. Be prepared to give an oral summary.

1. If you were the narrator of this story, what would you say to your grandfather when the keys were found?

2. If you were the grandfather, what would you say to the grandson at the end of the story?

3. The lost keys can be understood as a symbol. What do they symbolize?

4. Thinking back to the article "How to Grow Old and Stay Young," would you consider the grandfather to be an optimist or a pessimist? Explain your answer.

YOUTH
IN ACTION

These days, many people around the world are taking action through volunteer activities. Some people volunteer to work on environmental issues; others volunteer to help the less fortunate, while still others volunteer to raise money or campaign for change. In this unit you will learn how young people are taking action by volunteering their time on several important issues.

READING ONE

➤ BEFORE YOU BEGIN

1. This reading is an interview focusing on child labor. What do you know about child labor? Try answering these questions before you begin to read.

   a. How many working children are there in the world today?

   b. What are some reasons why children work?

   c. How young are they?

   d. How are they treated?

2. Now read the title and skim the reading looking for words in italics, names of people and places. Finally, read the first and last sentences of the reading. What additional information have you found out about this reading from skimming?

➤ AS YOU READ

Skim "Youth Takes Action Against Child Labor" to get an idea of what it is about.

YOUTH TAKES ACTION AGAINST CHILD LABOR
from *New Internationalist*

1   Iqbal Masih of Pakistan became a child laborer in 1986 when his parents offered to send him to a carpet manufacturer in exchange for a small loan. He was four years old. Like thousands of young children in his country, Iqbal was abused: chained to a loom[1] for 12 hours a day, six days a week, making entire carpets for pennies. The children   5 were malnourished, unable to go to school and not allowed to talk among themselves as they worked. They even slept next to their looms. The repetitious work often left their young fingers disfigured. Despite their long hours of work, their owners often hit and fined the children for not working fast enough or for making mistakes. The   10 fines, after years of work there, would put the children deeper in debt[2] than when they first arrived.

---

[1] *loom:* a machine for weaving carpets or cloth
[2] *debt:* money that is owed

2   In 1992, after six years of making carpets, Iqbal heard of an organization called the Bonded Labor Liberation Front that worked against child labor. Although virtually imprisoned by his owner, Iqbal managed to contact the group, and through their help he regained his freedom. Only 10 years old, he then committed his life to freeing other children. In 1994, he traveled to the United States to speak about the exploitation of children in the carpet industry. Full of hope and determination, Iqbal worked tirelessly on behalf of the children; however, he paid with his life for his dedication. Shortly after Iqbal returned to Pakistan, an assassin[3] fatally shot him in the head. No one has ever been convicted of Iqbal's murder.

3   After reading a Canadian newspaper article on Iqbal's case, 12-year-old Craig Kielburger of Toronto, Canada, wanted to do something on behalf of child laborers. He convinced his parents to allow him to travel to Asia to meet with carpet makers. When Craig returned, he sprang into action. He spoke with his classmates and local human rights organizations. With other students, they used the Internet to gather more information. Soon Craig led an effort to form the international group *Free the Children*.

4   *Interviewer:* Explain the concept behind the organization you started.

5   *Craig:* Free the Children is an international movement made up of young people ranging in age from 8 to 18. Basically it's an organization that tries to free children from abuse and exploitation; for example, those who are working as child soldiers, or those who have been sold into bondage[4] to work. Although *Free the Children* spends much of its time trying to help children in poorer countries, it also works to free children in Canada and the United States from the idea that they are powerless, that they are not old enough or capable enough to be involved in the decision making process. So we try to free these children also by giving them a voice.

6   *Interviewer:* What have you found most difficult in creating this organization?

7   *Craig:* The single biggest problem we've had is adults who will not

---

[3] *assassin:* a person who kills (assassinates) an important or famous person
[4] *bondage:* slavery

take us seriously, who think that because we are young we will oversimplify the issue of child labor and not do our research. Many of our members are as young as nine or ten years old but everyone does their research as well as taking action. 50

8   *Interviewer:* Why did the life of Iqbal Masih make such an impression on you?

9   *Craig:* Well, Iqbal was 12 years old and I was also 12 at that point, and so basically, I looked at my life and I looked at his and saw 55 the similarities and differences. After reading the article I realized we both had the same dreams, we both talked about the same things. The big thing that shocked me were the differences. I'd always thought, well, slavery, bonded labor, it's something out of the eighteenth and nineteenth centuries—it's been abolished, it 60 no longer exists.

10   *Interviewer:* So, you spoke about it in school and started a movement.

11   *Craig:* Exactly. I began doing research on the issue and then took what I knew and went to my class. I said: "This is what I want 65 to do—who wants to help?" From there it began to expand. Free the Children started as a group of 20 kids in Thornhill, a suburb of Toronto. Now we have groups in Canada, the U.S., Australia, Brazil, we have young people involved in Singapore, we get calls from Hong Kong, the United Arab Emirates, all 70 around the world.

12   *Interviewer:* Did you have any specific ideas on how to tackle the problem of child labor when you began?

13   *Craig:* There are over 250 million working children today between the ages of 5 and 14, all of them working in various situations 75 and conditions so child labor is a difficult problem to address, that's for sure. But that can't be used as an excuse not to take action. Consumer pressure can change things. In Pakistan, for example, consumer pressure resulted in the Government raising the amount they spent on primary education from one per cent 80 of the national budget to nearly three per cent, and building more than a thousand literacy centers. Even companies are beginning to take action in response to the pressure. Young people are beginning to realize their power.

14 *Interviewer:* Do you see yourself as a child worker? 85

15 *Craig:* No [he laughs], I see myself as a volunteer. We're a group of young people who volunteer to give up some of our spare time to work on this issue. We're not against children working— we're against children being abused and exploited.

16 *Interviewer:* Why do you think the organization has taken off the 90
way it has?

17 *Craig:* Well, I've met children who work 12 hours a day in agri- culture or sweatshops[5] or fighting a war, yet on the other extreme in North America, Europe and Australia are children who are given no responsibility and no chance to get involved. I think the 95
reason why Free the Children has grown so quickly is that we've given young people those opportunities. It's a challenge they can rise to. We have a girl of 12 from Ottawa, Canada, Laura Hannant, who just got back from giving the keynote address at an International Child Welfare Conference in the U.S.—before that 100
she was in South Africa and Holland. It just shows what young people can do when they're given the chance.

18 *Interviewer:* What do your parents think about all this?

19 *Craig:* I have very understanding parents. At the point where I was planning a seven-week trip to India and Pakistan last year at the 105
age of 13 they were pretty concerned—up to then my parents wouldn't even let me take the subway by myself, let alone travel to a different continent. But once they found out it was safe and well organized they let me go.

20 *Interviewer:* Where do you go from here? Will normal life ever 110
resume?

21 *Craig:* In a way I still consider this a normal kind of life. I will always stay involved with the issue of child labor to some extent. But it's young people who run Free the Children and eventually I will move on. Actually, when I'm older I hope to 115
work for Medecins Sans Frontieres[6], an organization I respect highly because it works on problems that are the world's responsibility. That's the thing about child labor, too—these are the world's children and the world's responsibility.

---

[5] *sweatshop:* a place where people work in bad or dangerous conditions for very low pay
[6] *Medecins Sans Frontieres:* Doctors Without Borders, an organization of doctors who volunteer to serve anywhere in the world

➤ GETTING THE MAIN IDEA

Read these statements. Which one best expresses the point of this interview?

a. _____ Child workers like Iqbal Masih are being freed through the organization Free the Children.

b. _____ Craig Kielburger and other young people are taking action through Free the Children.

c. _____ Adults are impressed by the volunteer efforts of youth like Craig Keilburger.

➤ VOCABULARY IN CONTEXT

Find each word in the reading (the paragraph is in brackets [ ]). Use context clues to guess the meaning of the word. Circle *a* or *b*.

1. abused [1]
   a. treated badly
   b. lost

2. repetitious [1]
   a. boring
   b. done many times

3. exploitation [2]
   a. unfair treatment
   b. families

4. dedication [2]
   a. trip
   b. hard work

5. convicted [2]
   a. found guilty
   b. convinced

6. tackle [12]
   a. begin to fight
   b. read about

► TAKING A CLOSER LOOK

Read "Youth Takes Action Against Child Labor" again, focusing on details. Are these sentences true (**T**) or false (**F**)? Underline a sentence or phrase in the reading that supports your answer. When you finish, compare your answers with your classmates' answers.

1. _____ Iqbal Masih earned money to attend school by weaving carpets.

2. _____ The owner of the carpet business owed a lot of money to Iqbal.

3. _____ Iqbal was freed through the organization Free the Children.

4. _____ Iqbal was 12 years old when he was shot.

5. _____ Free the Children is an international movement.

6. _____ According to Craig, the biggest problem for Free the Children is adults who won't do their research.

7. _____ Craig had never heard of slavery before he met Iqbal.

8. _____ Free the Children is not against children working.

9. _____ Craig's parents support his volunteer work.

10. _____ Craig believes everyone is responsible for child exploitation.

➤ **READING SKILL: Words that signal change**

Signal words connect information in a reading text. Some signal words tell the reader that a new point is going to be made about the main idea. Some of them are *yet, although, despite, but, however,* and *while.* A good reading strategy is to notice the signal word and underline the new information as you read. Then pause to process the information before reading on.

➤ **READING SKILL PRACTICE: Words that signal change**

Read these sentences from the interview. Circle the signal word and underline the new information. Pause to process the new information. Then circle *a* or *b.*

Example:

This sentence from the reading is an example of how a signal word is used to introduce a new point. The signal word *despite* is circled. We already know that the children work long hours. The new information is underlined. Answer *b* is circled because it expresses the new point the writer is making.

(Despite) long hours of work, the <u>owners often hit and fined the children for not working fast enough or for making mistakes.</u> (paragraph 1)

The new information is that _____.

  a. the owners hit the children to make them work long hours

  (b.) the owners hit the children even though they worked long hours

  1. Although virtually imprisoned by his owner, Iqbal managed to contact the group . . . (paragraph 2)

     The new information is that_____.

     a. Iqbal was almost a slave

     b. Iqbal contacted the group

  2. . . . Iqbal worked tirelessly on behalf of the children; however, he paid with his life for his dedication. (paragraph 2)

     The new information is that _____.

     a. Iqbal was killed

     b. Iqbal worked hard for the children

3. Although *Free the Children* spends much of its time trying to help children in poorer countries, it also works to free children in Canada and the United States from the idea that they are powerless, . . . (paragraph 5)

The new information is that _____.

a. *Free the Children* helps children in poorer countries

b. *Free the Children* also helps children in richer countries

4. Child labor is a very difficult problem to address, that's for sure. But that can't be used as an excuse not to take action. (paragraph 13)

The new information is that_____.

a. it is hard to fight child labor

b. we have to fight child labor

5. I've met children who work 12 hours a day . . . , yet, on the other extreme, in North America, Europe, and Australia are children who are given no responsibility and no chance to get involved. (paragraph 17)

The new information is that_____.

a. some children have nothing useful to do

b. some children work 12 hours a day

➤ INTERACTIVE JOURNAL RESPONSE

Choose one of the following questions and write a response. Be prepared to give an oral summary.

1. Who do you think is responsible for Iqbal Masih's death? Explain.

2. Craig Kielburger could be seen as a representative of the Millennial Generation you read about in Chapter 1. Why? Do you think it is important for young people like Craig to take action for world issues such as child labor? Why or why not?

3. What more do you want to know about child labor? Write down two or three questions you would like answered. Now use the Internet to look up information on child labor. Read the information and write up answers to your questions.

READING TWO

➤ BEFORE YOU BEGIN

Answer these questions with a partner.

1. What are some activities do you associate with volunteering?

   a. reading to old people or the sick

   b. _____

   c. _____

   d. _____

2. What are some of the volunteer activities and organizations you have heard about in your country or your community? Tell what you know about them.

3. Read the title and skim the reading. From your skimming, what do you think this reading is about?

➤ AS YOU READ

Skim "Teens Talking to Teens" to get an idea of what the article is about.

TEENS TALKING TO TEENS
by Ingrig Mager, from *The UNESCO Courier*

1   Ask a group of people what volunteering means and you're likely to get a whole range of answers. For some people, it conjures up   5 images of people helping the less fortunate—providing assistance to children, the ill, the elderly, or the blind. For other people, volunteering means campaigning for change, such as   10 getting involved with a local environmental pressure group[1] to stop logging in a rainforest, or supporting a global drive to abolish landmines. For still others, volunteering is about the struggle for

---

[1] *environmental pressure group:* a group of people who take action to protect the environment

survival; for example, working at a homeless shelter, or raising money for victims of a natural disaster such as an earthquake or flood to ensure the essentials of everyday life. 15

2   Whatever form it takes, voluntary activity stands apart form paid work or leisure in three ways. Firstly, it is not carried out primarily for monetary gain. Secondly, it is carried out freely; by definition, there is no coercion by other people. Thirdly, volunteering must 20 benefit the community although it can also be rewarding for the volunteer, often in intangible[2] ways. The personal satisfaction, the real-world exposure, the "chance to give something back," as dozens of volunteers put it, is enough.

3   Today, young people are becoming very involved in volunteer 25 activities. No one can say exactly how many are involved overall, but some estimate that on average between 15% and 25% of teens are taking action in some form or other around the world today.

4   Take, for example, this story from Slovenia.

5   The phone rings for two high school volunteers, Tina and Jana at 30 the Youth Counseling Center in Ljubljana, the capital of Slovenia. "I'll get it!" says Jana. "This is 'Teens Talking to Teens' . . . ". This popular telephone hotline[3], started by teens for other troubled teens, began in 1993. But what's so special about this self-financing project? The people answering the phones aren't professionals but 14- to 18- 35 year-olds. Pairs of them are on duty every day from three to five in the afternoon, except weekends and vacations. At first, they were teenagers from the neighborhood. Then their schoolmates and friends of friends started pitching in[4]. Today, they number about 50.

6   "Everybody knows our phone number," says Nina. "It's posted in 40 the schools. Most callers are high school students. Some of them think we'll do their math homework." But that's not what the hotline is there for. "Mothers call us too," says Daniel, "when they have reason to believe their children are taking drugs. We of course do not have the expertise to advise on such cases but we've got a good file of special 45 institutions we can refer them to. And when the situation looks serious, we transfer the call to the professional staff." The volunteers have been advised that drugs are a matter for experts, and they agree.

---

[2] *intangible*: emotional, not material
[3] *hotline*: a special telephone number to call for help
[4] *pitch in*: help out

7   Rees, who has been volunteering since the group first began, says the best thing about the hotline is that it gives teenagers a chance to speak freely about school, parents, and the other issues they're bothered about. "It's different from going to shrinks[5]."

8   Adults, including center director Ljubo Raicevic, psychologist Natsa Fabjan, and educator Lili Raicevic, keep a low profile[6]. Their role is limited to training and supervising the volunteers. The teens say that answering the questions is not easy. "Sometimes you feel powerless; also, it's hard to know whether you really understand the caller's problem," says Andreja. If somebody calls several times, you eventually figure out what's really bothering them. But most people call just once, and you wonder whether you said the right thing." Nejc adds. "The best ideas always occur to you after hanging up! So, we tell ourselves that the main thing is to talk, if only to take the caller's mind off his or her dark thoughts."

9   Why do these young people spend hours on the phone with strangers? Maja, who is still a minor[7], has already been listening and counseling for three years. "The high school sent me here," she says. "They told me I was too talkative, and thought that talking on the phone would do me good. This volunteer group has given me something to focus on in my life; moreover, I've met lots of nice people here. We train together and go out together. We've all become friends."

10   The young volunteers are devoted to helping others, but they also get something out of the experience. For some, the hotline is a means to keep loneliness at bay[8]. For others, it satisfies their need for freedom and self assertion. "They're emerging from childhood and want to take on responsibilities, but people often tell them they're too young. Here, they're taken seriously. Volunteering gives them a chance to make the transition between play and work," says the center's director, an educator and psychotherapist by training. Furthermore, it provides them with opportunities to take action and gives them a voice in the real world.

11   The volunteers say that since they've started "talking to teens," they have become aware of other people's problems and can settle their own more easily. For example, Stela, who joined the group

---

[5] *shrink:* an informal term for psychiatrist, psychotherapist, or counselor
[6] *keep a low profile:* not say much about what one thinks or knows
[7] *a minor:* a young person under the legal age to drink, drive, vote, etc.
[8] *to keep [something] at bay:* to keep something away

when she was 13, eventually shared her problem—a serious conflict
with her parents—with her new friends.   85

12   The professional staff members have also had to work on themselves
and mature at the same time as the teens. "The idea of the volunteer
phone line came from them," says Raicevic. "At first, we were
reluctant to let them do it because they were stepping into an area
traditionally reserved for professionals and adults like us. But we   90
told ourselves that without young people, their influence and ideas,
we could never succeed. Why not let them take part in making
decisions and get involved? The 8,000 or so phone calls received
since the hotline opened in 1993 proves they can."

➤GETTING THE MAIN IDEA

Read these statements. Which best expresses the author's main idea?

a. _____ Teens can play an important role in volunteer activities today.

b. _____ Adults believe young people make good volunteers.

c. _____ Volunteers are often in conflict these days.

➤VOCABULARY IN CONTEXT

Find each word in the reading (the paragraph is in brackets [ ]). Use context
clues to guess the meaning of the word. Circle a or b.

1. conjures up [1]
   a. gives an idea
   b. erases

2. abolish [1]
   a. get rid of
   b. use more

3. coercion [2]
   a. cooperation
   b. pressure

4. devoted [10]

   a. give all their time

   b. afraid of

5. transition [10]

   a. change

   b. money

6. reluctant [12]

   a. not willing

   b. happy

➤ TAKING A CLOSER LOOK

Read "Teens Talking to Teens" again, this time focusing on details. Choose *a* or *b*. Then underline a sentence or phrase which supports your answer. When you finish, compare your answers with your classmates' answers.

1. One reason people volunteer is because _____.

   a. they are pressured by others to do it

   b. they want to help others

2. Up to _____ of young people are volunteering around the world today.

   a. 12%

   b. 25%

3. The Youth Counseling Center discussed in the reading gets its money from _____.

   a. local high school teachers

   b. the Center itself

4. About _____ youth volunteers work at the Center.

   a. 14 to 18

   b. 50

5. The Center's hotline helps teens who _____.

   a. need advice on personal issues

   b. need help with their homework

6. Professional staff members at the Center give advice to _____.

   a. all teens who call

   b. only callers with very serious problems

7. Most callers _____ about their problem.

   a. only call one time

   b. make several calls

8. "Talking to Teens" gives volunteers a chance to _____.

   a. take on responsibilities and give advice to teens

   b. give professional advice on serious drug problems

➤ READING SKILL: Words that Signal More

Some signal words tell the reader that more information is coming about a point that has already been made—that supporting details such as examples or additional facts will follow. Some of these signal words are:

such as	also	moreover	furthermore
in addition	and	for instance	for example

There is no need to switch your mind to a new topic, so don't slow down—keep on reading at the same pace.

➤ READING SKILL PRACTICE: Words that Signal More

Read these sentences from the article. Circle the signal word(s) and underline the new information. Then circle *a* or *b*.

Example:
The volunteers have been duly advised that drugs are a matter for experts, and they agree. (paragraph 6)

The new information is _____.

   a. an additional fact

   b. an explanation

1. For other people, volunteering means campaigning for change, such as getting involved with a local environmental pressure group to stop logging in a rainforest, or supporting a global drive to abolish landmines. (paragraph 1)

    The new information is _____.

    a. additional facts

    b. examples

2. "Sometimes you feel powerless; also, it's hard to know whether you really understand the caller's problem," says Andreja. (paragraph 8)

    The new information is _____.

    a. an additional fact

    b. an example

3. This volunteer group has given me something to focus on in my life; moreover, I've met lots of nice people here. (paragraph 9)

    The new information is _____.

    a. an additional fact

    b. an example

4. For still others, volunteering is about the struggle for survival; for example, working at a homeless shelter, or raising money for victims of a natural . . . (paragraph 1)

    The new information is _____.

    a. additional facts

    b. examples

5. Volunteering gives them a chance to make the transition between play and work," . . . Furthermore, it provides them with opportunities to take action and gives them a voice in the real world. (paragraph 10)

    The new information is _____.

    a. additional facts

    b. explanations

 ➤COMMUNICATE

Some colleges and universities give academic credit for volunteer work.

   a. In small groups of four or five, discuss the pros and cons of this practice.

   b. Write the pros and cons in the chart below.

   c. Be prepared to present your pros and cons to other groups in your class.

Academic Credit for Volunteer Work	
Pros	**Cons**
1.	
2.	
3.	
4.	
5.	

Use the expressions from the Appendix on pages 211 and 212 to help you.

➤ INTERACTIVE JOURNAL RESPONSE

Choose one of these questions and write a response. Be prepared to give an oral summary.

1. Do you think the volunteer hotline the teens are operating is a good idea? Why or why not? Do you think there is a need for a similar hotline for students in your community?

2. Research a volunteer group in your community or use the Internet to look up a volunteer organization (non-governmental organization) that you would like to know more about. Find out the purpose of this group or organization and the actions they are taking.

3. Interview a teacher or another student. Find out if that person has ever done volunteer work. If so, how did the person benefit from the experience? If not, what kind of volunteer work would he or she like to do, if any?

MUSIC

Recorded music has raised people's spirits since the invention of audio recording. Developments in audio and video technology have inspired artists to explore their creativity and have provided new ways for music lovers to enjoy a whole range of music styles. While this development has allowed the music industry to enjoy commercial success on a global scale, it has also challenged the industry.

READING ONE

►BEFORE YOU BEGIN

1. What is your favorite kind of music? Why do you like it?

2. Read the title and skim the first and last paragraphs of the article. From the information you have gathered why do you think some people are attracted to the music of club culture?

►AS YOU READ

Skim "The Body and Soul of Club Culture" to get an idea of what the article is about.

THE BODY AND SOUL OF CLUB CULTURE
by Hillegonda C. Rietveld, from *The UNESCO Courier*

1   United on the dance floors around the world, revelers[1] of different ethnic backgrounds and ages dance wall-to-wall, sweating, smiling, and enjoying the DJ's clever acoustic tricks. The combination of loud, rhythmic music and visual effects heightens the collective spirit as the sound enters the crowd—machine rhythms, pounding   5 drums. The thudding beats the DJs produce generate a feeling of Utopia[2]; a dream they hope to make a reality through club culture.

2   Around the world DJs are creating their own music in dance clubs. It takes determination because for the past several decades what is known as "dance culture" or "club culture"—based on electronic   10 music and its derivatives[3]—has been dominated by the commercial recording industry. The industry has not only monopolized the club culture market but has continued to increase its share of total music sales (Figure 6.1).

3   More recently, though, the club culture crowd is tuning out to   15 what the recording giants have to offer and tuning in to what the DJs are creating. From Algeria to New Zealand youth has seized upon the DJs' rhythm and beat to express anger, love, aspiration[4], and

---

[1] *revelers:* people who are having fun
[2] *Utopia:* a perfect place where everyone is happy
[3] *derivatives:* things that developed from something else
[4] *aspiration:* a goal or aim in life

Figure 6.1

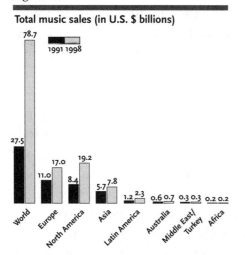

Total music sales (in U.S. $ billions)

1991 1998

World 78.7 27.5
Europe 17.0 11.0
North America 19.2 8.4
Asia 5.7 7.8
Latin America 1.2 2.3
Australia 0.6 0.7
Middle East/ Turkey 0.3 0.3
Africa 0.2 0.2

Source: International Federation of the Phonographic Industry

peace, as DJs spawn new creative sounds through the music of club culture. In the words of the renowned U.S. jazzman Charlie Parker, "Music is your own experience, your thoughts, your wisdom. If you don't live it, it won't come out of your horn." DJs and club goers around the world agree. [20] [25] [30]

4   But before delving into this global phenomenon, let's define it and go back through history to better understand the body and soul of club culture. To begin, the term "techno" is often referred to when describing anything with a thudding electronic beat, but not all club music is techno. Techno is actually part of an ever-expanding genre[5] generally called "electronic dance music." This genre spawns a constant stream of variants as the DJs recycle any kind of music or sound—from a train whistle to the chant of a Tibetan Lama—within the thudding of a four-beats-to-the-bar rhythm. Two of the major sub-genres of electronic dance music are techno and house. [35] [40]

5   The club culture surrounding the global techno scene is in some ways a reconfiguration of the disco culture of the 1970s. This era was perhaps best reflected in the American movie "Saturday Night Fever." Disco was commercial, but fun and funky. But as with all mainstream[6] music crazes, its popularity waned, and soon three great anti-commercial genres of popular music emerged around the world: reggae in Jamaica, punk in the U.K., and hip-hop in New York City. Although their sounds were different from disco sounds, the disco principle continued: playing a smooth mix of long single records to keep people "dancing all night long." [45] [50]

_____

[5] *genre*: a type or variety, for example a genre in music, art, literature, etc.

[6] *mainstream*: something most people like (music produced by the recording industry is mainstream)

6   In the late 1970s house music became popular. It originated in black and Latin discos in the U.S. And from it a sub-genre known as garage—slower and more gospel oriented than house—was spawned. Also techno, a cooler, more futuristic form of house music, emerged.

7   In the mid-80s, North American house and techno were exported to Europe. Gospel-oriented house music found an audience in Italy. Northern Europe favored cold, hard, techno; while the U.K. adopted all the sounds, mixing and adapting them for their clubs' crowds.

8   It wasn't long before yet another era of club culture began: "raves"—huge parties, often in illegal spaces, where DJs played through the night attracting thousands of paying participants. Raves became famous for law-breaking and violence and soon tougher laws began to close the rave clubs.

9   The late 1990s gave rise to "super clubs," with rationalized administration and marketing strategies. The clubs were profitable businesses, flying in the latest "star DJs" to play in a tightly controlled and regulated atmosphere.

10   Yet despite this commercial explosion and laws enforcing strict control over the club music scene, the dream of club culture's Utopia continues. DJs are still challenged by the creative potential club culture offers. They are also determined to remain detached from the global entertainment giants who control the music world (Figure 6.2). DJs are dedicated to producing music in new and creative ways, representing an escape from the mainstream music people usually hear on the radio. And for their fans, it's an idea that brings them back to the clubs night after night.

Figure 6.1

World market shares of the five major labels, 1998

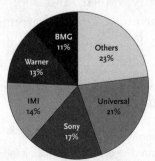

Source: Music Business International World Report 2000

➤ GETTING THE MAIN IDEA

Complete this summary of the main ideas with words from the list.

DJs   mainstream   phenomenon

club culture   monopolized   reconfiguration

Although _____ is a global _____ these days, it is really a
            (1)   (2)
_____ of the disco era of the 1970s. And even though the music indus-
      (3)
try has _____ the music of club culture for some time, _____
              (4)   (5)
around the world are determined to create alternatives to _____ music.
                                                                    (6)

➤ VOCABULARY IN CONTEXT

Find each word in the paragraph indicated in brackets [ ]. Use context clues to
guess the meaning of the word. Circle *a* or *b*.

1. determination [2]

   a. money

   b. long, hard work

2. spawn [3, 4, 6]

   a. create, develop

   b. fight against

3. recycle [4]

   a. move

   b. re-use

4. delve into [4]

   a. look at

   b. leave

5. waned [5]

   a. decreased

   b. grew

6. detached [10]

    a. closed

    b. separated

➤TAKING A CLOSER LOOK

Read "The Body and Soul of Club Culture" again, focusing on details. Then choose *a*, *b*, or *c*. When you finish, compare your answers with your classmates' answers.

1. The music of club culture has been controlled by_____.

    a. DJs

    b. the music industry

    c. young people

2. Club music was first introduced in _____.

    a. Britain

    b. the United States

    c. Spain

3. Young people like the music _____ are producing because it expresses their feelings and ideas.

    a. DJs

    b. entertainment giants

    c. mainstream artists

4. Techno music is just one kind of _____.

    a. club culture

    b. electronic dance music

    c. reggae

5. Club culture may have originated in _____.

    a. thudding sounds

    b. house music

    c. the disco era

6. Reggae, punk, and hip-hop were _____ types of music when first introduced.

   a. mainstream

   b. alternative

   c. fashionable

7. _____ made it difficult for raves to continue.

   a. The recording industry

   b. Tough laws

   c. Super clubs

8. DJs want to produce music _____.

   a. that is creative

   b. that is mainstream

   c. for the recording giants

➤ READING SKILL: Using Graphic Aids

Graphic aids—tables, graphs, charts, and diagrams—are used to illustrate, summarize, or support the ideas of a reading. Graphs, charts, and diagrams are called "figures" in the reading. Tables are called "tables."

These guidelines will help you read and understand graphic aids:

- Read the title of the graphic aid. The title tells you what information is being presented.

- Read any words, phrases, or sentences in the visual aid. Examine the information in each part of it.

- Make some general comparisons of the information in the graphic aid. Note the differences, the similarities, and the trends it shows.

- Draw a general conclusion.

- Check the source and date. The source of the information usually appears at the bottom along with the date. The source tells where the data come from. The date tells you how recent the information is. Both the source and the date help you judge how reliable the information is.

➤ **READING SKILL PRACTICE: Using Graphic Aids**

Part A: Reading a Bar Graph

Study the information in Figure 6.1 on page 87. Then answer these questions.

1. Read the title. What is the bar graph about? Check the best choice:

   a. _____ the amount of money made from music sales each year since 1991.

   b. _____ the increase in world music sales between 1991 and 1998.

   c. _____ a comparison of music sales by region in 1991 and 1998.

2. Read the column headings along the bottom of the bar graph. Now follow each bar to its end with your finger and read the number.

3. Make comparisons. Now fill in the blanks.

   a. World music sales have _____ by nearly US$2 billion a year between 1991 and 1998.

   b. The largest increase in sales occurred in _____.

   c. There was no increase in music sales both in the _____ and _____.

4. Study the information on the bar again. Then choose the statement that gives the best general conclusion.

   a. _____ The music industry has experienced substantial growth since 1991.

   b. _____ The music industry has grown worldwide.

   c. _____ Africa has not contributed to the growth in the music industry.

5. What is the source of the data? _____

Part B: Reading a Pie Graph

Study the information in Figure 6.2 on page 88. Then answer these questions.

1. Read the title. What is the pie graph about? Check the best choice:

   a. _____ the percentage of money each of the major labels made in 1998

   b. _____ the percentage of music sales of each of the major labels in relation to all music sales in 1998

   c. _____ the percentage of consumers who bought music from the five major labels in 1998

2. Read the information written on each section of the pie.

3. Make comparisons. Now fill in the blanks.

   a. Of the 5 major labels _____ had the largest percent of record sales.

   b. _____ had the smallest percent of record sales.

   c. All other record labels combined had _____ record sales than any one of the 5 major labels.

4. Study the information on the graph again. Then choose the statement that gives the best general conclusion.

   a. _____ There is fairly close competition between the five major labels.

   b. _____ Universal is much more popular than the other major labels.

   c. _____ 1998 was a bad year for BMG.

5. What is the source of the data? _____

➤ INTERACTIVE JOURNAL RESPONSE

Choose one of these questions and write a response. Be prepared to give an oral summary.

1. Charlie Parker (U.S. jazzman 1920–1955) once said, "Music is your own experience, your thoughts, your wisdom. If you don't live it, it won't come out of your horn." What did he mean by that statement?

2. Choose a genre of music that interests you. Research the history. Does the music convey a message or an opinion? Has the music had an effect on society? Has it had an effect on you of other fans you know?

READING TWO

➤ BEFORE YOU BEGIN

1. Work with a partner. Fill in the chart.

   a. Where do you usually get information about the latest recordings by your favorite musicians?

   b. If you wanted to listen to a CD without buying it where would you go?

	record shop	friends	the Internet	other
You				
a.				
b.				
Your Partner				
a.				
b.				

2. Read the title and skim the first paragraph of Reading Two. What do you think this reading is about?

➤ AS YOU READ

Skim "Piracy in the Music Industry" to get an idea of what the article is about.

PIRACY IN THE MUSIC INDUSTRY

1   Sound recording piracy—the unauthorized duplication of the sounds of legitimate recordings—has adversely affected the recording industry since its earliest days. The first signs of concern in the recording industry came in the 1960s with the development of sound recording technology. This opened the doors to the pirating and distribution of cassette tapes, but because pirating on ordinary tapes was difficult and the resulting sound quality was often poor, the threat to the music industry was not great. The advent of digital technology in the 1980s, however, sparked a spiraling rate of piracy. And more recently with the accessibility of music files over the

Internet, piracy in the digital era has hit the music industry where it hurts.

2   Cassette piracy has become a major criminal activity in many   20
parts of the world. Cassette piracy in Africa and other developing
regions of the world is increasingly widespread. In many African
countries where the daily income is less than two dollars, the
demand for pirated tapes is high (Table 6.3). Street prices of pirate
cassettes in these countries range from $2 to $5 compared to legitimate   25
recordings which sell for between $7 and $10 per tape. And as the
demand for pirated tapes increases, the potential profits become
enormous.

Table 6.3

Music cassettes and piracy in selected African countries (1998)

Country	Number of music cassettes sold (millions)	Retail value (U.S. $ millions)	Piracy level (%)
Ghana	7.4	25	10-25
Kenya	0-4	2	over 50
South Africa	7.3	196	10-25
Zimbabwe	1.5	9	25-50

Source: International Federation of the Phonographic Industry

3   Unlike a record company, the pirate bears none of the initial cost
of searching for talent, creating, producing, marketing, and publicizing   30
a recording, which can add up to millions of dollars. Nor does a
pirate pay union fees, artists, back-up vocalists, royalties or taxes.
Beyond the cost of purchasing a single commercial copy for use as a
master, the pirate incurs only a per-unit manufacturing cost of well
under a dollar. Breaching[1] copyright laws in these countries is seen   35
not so much as an illegal act but as a way to beat down the cost for
the consumer and create profitable opportunities for the network of
pirates working in these regions.

4   More recently, CD piracy has also become a lucrative business.
With the advent of digital technology, duplicating legitimate recordings   40
has become simpler and the sound quality next to perfect. Figure 6.4
shows countries with the highest CD piracy figures in 1998. And not

---

[1] *breaching:* breaking

only are pirate recordings of CDs showing up on the streets but music from the leading artists to much lesser known artists can now be downloaded on the Internet using the MP3 format. This audio 45 format allows individuals to compress audio CDs into small files that can then be distributed. Just click, download, and listen. All that is needed is a modem, a phone line, and a computer. There are no additional costs other than the phone bill. It is quick and easy to download and distribute music files. 50

Figure 6.4

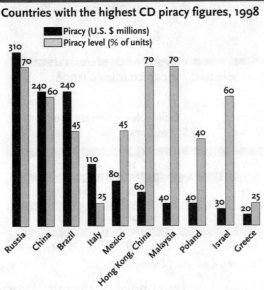

Countries with the highest CD piracy figures, 1998

- Piracy (U.S. $ millions)
- Piracy level (% of units)

Source: International Federation of the Phonographic Industry

5   And while enthusiasts of MP3 claim they are not actually stealing intellectual property[2] held by the music 55 industry or the recording artists, those in the industry argue it is a clear breach of copyright laws and a lack of 60 respect for the legislative regulations in the industry and for the recording artists themselves. Frank 65 Creighton, vice president of the Recording Industry Association of America (RIAA) says, "Downloading an MP3 is no different than walking into a record store, putting a CD in your pocket, and walking out without paying." As a result, the 70 industry has taken several steps to gain control of the situation.

6   In their attempts, the industry has campaigned to shut down Internet sites that illegally distribute copyrighted music. The big five record labels EMI, BMG, Sony, Universal, and Warner, and 1400 record producers and distributors in 70 countries have taken action 75 against hundreds of sites for the infringement of laws in more than 20 countries worldwide. They have not only sent threatening letters to Webmasters (the online sites that procure[3] the music) demanding

---

[2] *intellectual property:* ideas, words, or other written work that is the creation of an individual

[3] *procure:* get hold of

immediate closure of their sites, but in some cases, have taken MP3
pirates to court. Creighton supports such action by claiming that   80
"Internet pirates are making available—illegally—a huge range of
music from top international acts to national chart-topping artists
singing in their local languages." He estimates there are over 1 million
illegal music files posted on the Internet that infringe copyright laws
and need to be shut down immediately.   85

7   Enthusiasts of MP3 technology on the other hand, say they are not
stealing intellectual property and claim there is nothing really illegal
about using the technology to download a couple of songs for free
without depending on the old-fashioned music industry. They deny
allegations[4] that MP3 is illegal. They argue that it is simply an audio   90
compression file format and by itself is not illegal or legal, it depends
how it is implemented. Fans of MP3 say it is already the de facto[5]
standard. There are more MP3 listeners, software programs, and
hardware devices than any other CD-quality audio format in the
world, and the technology is only going to expand in this area.   95

8   While the record labels say they are losing billions to MP3 piracy,
supporters of MP3 charge the music industry with over-inflating the
price of retail CDs. (They cost roughly a dollar to make but retail for
$10 and up.) They say MP3 technology exposes people to more
music who then buy CDs from bands they would never have heard   100
otherwise. In fact, they say artists and labels can make money by
employing MP3 technology because they have a world audience on
the Internet at little or no cost. While the majority of MP3 users may
be right that the MP3 is not illegal in itself, they do need to recognize
copyright laws. The forces on each side are determined to fight for   105
what they believe are their rights. Only time will tell which side wins.

---

[4] *allegations*: claims
[5] *de facto*: already common

►GETTING THE MAIN IDEA

Complete this summary of the main ideas with words from the list.

cassette tapes   Internet   over-inflating   right

developing   MP3 format   piracy

_____ has affected the music industry for many years. Sound recording
          (1)

piracy of _____ has become increasingly widespread in _____
              (2)   (3)

regions of the world, while piracy on the _____ has become a serious
                                                  (4)

threat in developed regions of the world. The music industry claims that the

_____ is illegal and is destroying the recording industry. Enthusiasts of
        (5)

this digital technology claim they have the _____ to use it and that the
                                                      (6)

industry is _____ the price of retail CDs.
                 (7)

►VOCABULARY IN CONTEXT

Find each word in the reading (the paragraphs are in brackets [ ]). Use context
clues to guess the meaning of the word. Circle *a* or *b*.

1. adversely [1]

   a. favorably

   b. unfavorably

2. advent [1]

   a. start

   b. end

3. spiraling [1]

   a. increasing

   b. decreasing

4. lucrative [4]

   a. well-paid

   b. dangerous

5. infringement [6]

   a. passing

   b. breaking

6. implemented [7]

   a. used

   b. stolen

➤ TAKING A CLOSER LOOK

Read "Piracy in the Music Industry" again, focusing on details. Are these sentences true (**T**) or false (**F**)? When you finish, compare your answers with your classmates' answers.

1. _____ The sound on pirated cassette tapes was often very good.

2. _____ Copying cassette tapes provides little income for music pirates in developing countries.

3. _____ People in the business of pirating CDs are making lots of money.

4. _____ The development of digital technology has made the pirating of CDs easy.

5. _____ You need MP3 to download music from the Internet.

6. _____ Some music websites have distributed music without paying copyright fees.

7. _____ MP3 users say the music industry is making money through MP3 technology.

8. _____ Responsibility for copyright permission has created the biggest problem in downloading and distributing music on the Internet.

➤ READING SKILL PRACTICE: Reading a Table

Like graphs, tables are mainly used to present the findings of research in the form of statistical information. Writers use tables to provide numerical evidence for statements they make.

Part A

Study the information in Table 6.3. Then answer these questions.

1. Read the title. What is the table about? Check the best choice:

    a. _____ the sales of music cassettes and percent piracy in African countries

    b. _____ the amount of money made through piracy in several African countries

    c. _____ the African countries with the highest piracy level in 1998

2. Read the column headings. What do the column headings tell you?

    _____

3. Read the row headings. From which countries have the data been collected?

4. Make comparisons. Now fill in the blanks.

    a. Although Ghana sold _____ cassettes than South Africa, their

       retail sales were much _____ than South Africa's.

    b. Kenya sold the _____ number of cassettes but had the

       _____ piracy level.

    c. Zimbabwe and Kenya made much _____ money than Ghana and

       South Africa because of _____ piracy levels.

5. Study Table 6.3. Then choose the statement that gives the best conclusion.

    a. _____ South Africans have more purchasing power.

    b. _____ The piracy level in Africa is high.

    c. _____ Very few legitimate cassettes are bought in Kenya.

6. Where do the data come from?

    _____

Part B

    a. Study Figure 6.4. Review the "Guidelines for Reading Graphic Aids" from Reading One.

    b. Then answer these questions.

1. What is Figure 6.4 about?

_____

2. Make 3 comparisons about the bar graph.

    a. _____

    b. _____

    c. _____

3. What conclusion can you draw from the information in Figure 6.4?

_____

4. What is the source of the data?

_____

➤ COMMUNICATE

Do you think people have the right to use the audio format MP3 to download music over the Internet? Why or why not?

Work with a small group.

1. Write down three or four reasons *for* and three or four reasons *against* the use of MP3.

2. When you finish, join with another group and compare your reasons. Your teacher may assign you one side and then ask you to present your side of the argument.

Reasons For MP3	*Reasons Against MP3*
_____	_____
_____	_____
_____	_____
_____	_____

Use the expressions on pages 211 and 212 to help you.

➤ INTERACTIVE JOURNAL RESPONSE

Choose one of these questions and write a response. Be prepared to give an oral summary.

1. Have you ever bought or would you ever buy pirated music recordings? Why or why not?

2. Many students say they can't afford to buy compact discs, claiming they are overpriced. They say the recording industry is making too much money and that using the audio format MP3 is one way to fight back against the music establishment. What is your reaction to this?

3. An array of new audio and video gadgets and equipment become available every year. What do you know about the latest developments and trends in digital equipment? What product would you like to buy? Are there any ethical or legal issues involved in purchasing or using this product? Research a product that interests you.

VALUE
OF WORK

Work can be good and it is necessary, but when work becomes all-consuming, we lose our freedom to manage our lives as we wish. Sometimes we need to reflect on the value of work and how it can affect the rest of our lives.

READING ONE

➤ BEFORE YOU BEGIN

1. List three reasons why it is important for people to work.

   a. _____

   b. _____

   c. _____

2. What kind of job would you like to have in the future? Why?

➤ READING SKILL: Inferences from Photographs and Titles

Inferences are conclusions made by a reader based on information in and around a reading passage. Readers can infer something about the reading from the words used in the title and from accompanying photographs.

➤ READING SKILL PRACTICE: Inferences from Photographs and Titles

1. Study the photograph that illustrates Reading One. What exactly do you see? Write three or four of the most important details.

   Example: A woman using a computer at home

   a. _____

   b. _____

   c. _____

   d. _____

2. Read the title. Look up "invasion" if you are not sure of its meaning.

3. From the photograph and the title, what can you infer about the article? What do you think it will be about?

   a. _____ how much fun it is working from home

   b. _____ the impact work has on our lives

   c. _____ the importance of work

➤ **AS YOU READ**

Skim "The Invasion of Work" to get an idea of what it is about.

THE INVASION OF WORK

1   For many people, technological advances have changed the traditional idea of the nine-to-five workday. Now the workweek has exploded from forty to fifty and sometimes sixty or more hours. With computers and the Internet at our fingertips whenever and wherever we go, work is suited perfectly to 24-hours-a-day, 7-days-a-week. Dubbed the "24/7" working world, this new way of work has resulted in long hours and blurred boundaries between work and home. The use of e-mail, laptops, cellular phones, the Internet, and hand-held electronic personal organizers has created a direct link between work and personal life. It is now possible to go to the park, lay a quilt in the shade, lean up against a tree trunk with a laptop and cell phone, and do your business for the day. It is true—thanks to technology, people can choose where and when they perform at least some of their work. But as people have increased the number of hours they spend at work, both in the office and at home, they are now starting to reflect on the effect 24/7 has on their lives. In today's complex and fast-paced world, working wherever and whenever we need to has its advantages, but it also has some disadvantages.

2   Mary Wohlfarth, executive editor for I.D. magazine, a bimonthly publication devoted to working trends, claims that although people like the idea of having access to the office while away from their

desk, they feel uncomfortable with the new style of workplace. Wohlfarth recalls one magazine article about a virtual office[1] experiment done by a Los Angeles advertising company. "Everyone had laptop computers and cell phones," she says. Employees could set up wherever and whenever they wanted. The advertising company was confident all the people in the experiment would favor this new kind of work environment, however, the experiment drew mixed reactions. "Over half of the people in the experiment said they preferred having an office and a permanent desk to go to every day. They also said they missed seeing their colleagues," Wohlfarth says.

3   When you're in a park or café, you don't have privacy, and people need private space to do concentrated work. Likewise, when you work for a company, you like to come in and actually interact with your colleagues occasionally. The Los Angeles advertising company has since made their work place more flexible, allowing for private and public workspace to suit employees' needs, says Wohlfarth. "The whole idea of the modern work place is that things aren't hard and fast[2]. The workspace of the future is flexible. But it's a step back from the virtual office."

4   While employees seem to reject the virtual office potential of the 24/7 working world, the majority of people working in offices are interested in using technology to connect them to the office from home, or when they're traveling. Consider the growing demand for Internet technologies for cars. According to research by GM and Ford, the number one and number two carmakers in the world, we are entering a new era of auto technology appropriately dubbed the "e-car." And it's suited perfectly to the 24-hours-a-day, 7-days-a-week working world. E-GM, the Internet technology division of GM, is leading the way in offering wireless Internet services in their cars through voice recognition software, which includes features such as e-mail, "personal calling" (allowing the driver to make voice-activated calls without an additional cellular contract), stock quotes, news headlines, and more. This technology ensures that today's workforce can tackle some of their duties in their cars before they even get into the office parking lot.

---

[1] *virtual office:* anywhere that people want to work with technology that lets them work as if in an office

[2] *things aren't hard and fast:* there are no specific rules, everything is flexible and can be changed when necessary

5   With technology expanding the world of work beyond office walls, the next logical step in the 24/7 work world is the introduction of flextime—working during non-traditional working hours. Once office space became more flexible, and the use of high-tech communication became more common, many companies began to offer employees the option of working their eight hours a day or forty hours a week any time they could fit them in, including the middle of the night and on Sundays. So it was only a question of when the 40-hour workweek would be broken. This happened most infamously with the dot-com companies, whose flexible working hours initially enabled employees to stay at work for longer periods.

6   Combine this with other companies fighting the clock to beat competitors in the current race for globalization, and today we find work is everywhere. Go to the café, and someone's in the corner peering into a laptop screen and talking on a cellular phone. At the bookstore, at the park, and in cars, people are busy incorporating work into their lives. After-work happy hours have turned into a setting where young executives discuss the next software development, cutting into the time families used to have together to eat dinner and talk about their days.

7   Some people see the lack of a barrier between work and home as benefiting their lives, while others see it as being detrimental. Freelance writer Jennifer Brock for one, believes that flextime has made her more productive and her life more fun. She says some of her best work comes to her while she's doing other things. "[My work] truly ceases to feel like work, because I can be standing in line for a coffee and thinking about that perfect word or line. When it comes to me, I simply sit down with my coffee and punch it into my cell phone and send it off to my computer at home."

8   Even though Brock bills by the hour, "with a stopwatch in hand," she likes to take things in bite-size pieces, and enjoys playing in the middle of the day. "I keep a notepad by my bed, and I get up at five a.m. to write. I can work when something hits me, and if my friend calls and asks if I want to see a matinee[3], I say, 'Sure!' But that's the beauty of flextime," says Brock.

9   Richard Hunt, director of sales and marketing for a publications company, takes advantage of the flextime and technology at his

---

[3] *matinee*: afternoon movie

company so he can spend more time with his three children. "One of the things I do now that I was never able to do before is drive my kids to school in the morning," Hunt says. "Before our office went on flextime, I seldom saw them for 15 minutes a day." Taking the kids to school means he doesn't get into the office until after 10 a.m., but that's perfectly fine with his boss. Hunt also comes home in time for dinner, and then goes back into the office once his kids go to bed.   105

                                                                            110

10   While executives like Hunt and freelancers like Brock are content with the lack of a line between work and personal life, there's a backlash[4] against the 24/7 work invasion in other sectors of the workforce. This is true especially among the young employees in dot-com start-ups[5] who, in the beginning, were keen to work long hours and liked the idea of the lack of separation between work and play.   115

11   Pamela Kruger, contributing editor of Fast Company magazine writes about the dilemma for employees at dot-com start-ups. "Now, many of these young employees are suffering from burnout[6]," Kruger says. "Also, there's a new group of employees entering the dot-com universe: adults in their 30s and 40s to whom the idea of listening to loud rap music and sitting at their computer terminal at 2 a.m. is anything but desirable." According to Kruger, where employees were once willing to sacrifice evenings and weekends for their company, they are now looking at quality of life issues. "Once the romance of a start-up is over, many employees discover that the sacrifices associated with working long hours aren't worth it. They come to realize after a while that they're spending most of their week nights working until 1 a.m., drinking coffee and eating junk." Kruger reports that many start-ups are getting the message, and changing to a more traditional 40-hour workweek.   120

                                                                            125

                                                                            130

12   In the end, employees don't seem to mind the 24/7 working world that's been woven into their lives through modern technology. To the contrary, the benefits of working from home, making the park a virtual office for an afternoon, or taking advantage of flextime   135

---

[4] *backlash:* a popular feeling against a formerly accepted belief or practice
[5] *dot-com start-up:* an Internet company in its early development stages
[6] *burnout:* to be exhausted because of work or working conditions, to dislike work a person once liked

to see an afternoon movie with a friend are welcome in most workplaces around the world. What isn't welcome is exercising these options in a way that overwhelms an individual's right to a   140 personal life.

➤ GETTING THE MAIN IDEAS

Complete this summary of the main ideas with words from the list.

virtual office   flextime   technology   personal

24/7   flexible working

Advances in _____ and the introduction of _____ hours, also
             (1)   (2)
known as _____ , has led to the _____ workweek. Although
         (3)   (4)
the idea of working in a _____ is attractive to employees, most still
                         (5)
want to draw a line between their working lives and their _____ lives.
                                                          (6)

➤ VOCABULARY IN CONTEXT

Find each word in the reading (the paragraph is in brackets [ ]). Use context clues to guess the meaning of the word. Circle *a* or *b*.

1. blurred [1]

   a. unclear

   b. definite

2. devoted to [2]

   a. against

   b. about

3. tackle [4]

   a. begin

   b. avoid

4. detrimental [7]

   a. good

   b. bad

5. sacrifice [11]

   a. give up

   b. share

6. contrary [12]

   a. opposite

   b. same

►TAKING A CLOSER LOOK

Read "The Invasion of Work" again, focusing on details. Are these sentences true (T) or false (F)? Underline a sentence or phrase in the reading that supports your answer. When you finish, compare your answers with your classmates' answers.

1. _____ Most people have 24 vacation days in 7 months—24/7.

2. _____ Technology makes it harder for people to work outside the office these days.

3. _____ According to Mary Wohlfarth, people do not like the idea of a permanent work place.

4. _____ The "e-car" makes it possible for people to do some of their work before they get to the office.

5. _____ Flextime allows people to work anywhere except at home.

6. _____ It was the dot-com start-ups that began the forty-hour workweek.

7. _____ After working very long hours, some of the young employees at dot-com start-ups became dissatisfied with their work situations.

8. _____ According to the reading, most employees want time for their personal lives.

➤ READING SKILL: Inferences from Words and Statements

Sometimes writers do not directly state what they want to say but instead provide the reader with clues—words and phrases that imply information without stating it. Readers can infer meaning and draw conclusions based on these clues. Inferences can also be made from the reader's own experience and previous knowledge.

What inferences can you make based on the information in Reading One?

Example:
Read the following sentence from paragraph 3:

The advertising company was confident all the people in the experiment would favor this new kind of work environment, however, the experiment drew mixed reactions.

What inference can you make based on the stated information?

  a. Everyone in the experiment liked the new work environment.

  b. Not everyone in the experiment liked the new work environment.

  c. No one in the experiment liked the new work environment.

The answer is *b*. We can infer that not everyone liked it because of the word "mixed," which implies different responses.

➤ READING SKILL PRACTICE: Inferences from Words and Statements

Choose the best inference for each sentence.

- Read the sentence and the three possible inferences.

- Find the sentence in the reading and look for additional context information.

- Check *a*, *b*, or *c*.

- In the paragraph, underline the clue(s) that helped you choose.

1. "But that's the beauty of flextime," says Brock. (paragraph 8)

  a. _____ Brock really likes flextime.

  b. _____ Brock thinks flextime is a chance to improve her beauty.

  c. _____ According to Brock, beauty is the reason to work.

2. While executives like Hunt and freelancers like Brock are content with the lack of a line between work and personal life, there's a backlash against the 24/7 work invasion in other sectors of the workforce. (paragraph 10)

   a. _____ All working people dislike the 24/7 working world.

   b. _____ Not everyone is as satisfied as Hunt and Brock about the 24/7 working world.

   c. _____ Hunt and Brock want to force other people into the 24/7 working world.

3. This is true especially among the young employees in dot-com start-ups who, in the beginning, were keen to work long hours and liked the idea of the lack of separation between work and play. (paragraph 10)

   a. _____ Young employees feel different about their job conditions than they did before.

   b. _____ Young employees want to work longer hours than they did before.

   c. _____ Being able to play at work has changed for young employees at dot-com start-ups.

4. Once the romance of a start-up is over, many employees discover that the sacrifices associated with working long hours aren't worth it. (paragraph 11)

   a. _____ Employees love dot-com start-ups because they can work many hours.

   b. _____ Once reality sets in, the long hours at dot-com start-ups may not be very attractive.

   c. _____ In reality, employees find dot-com start-ups attractive because of the long working hours.

5. Kruger reports that many start-ups are getting the message. (paragraph 11)

   a. _____ Many start-ups realize there is a problem and are taking action.

   b. _____ Many start-ups rely heavily on e-mail for communication in the office.

   c. _____ Most start-ups do not know what to do about the problem.

➤INTERACTIVE JOURNAL RESPONSE

Choose one of the following questions and write a response. Be prepared to give an oral summary.

1. Explain the concept of the 24/7 working world. Would you like this type of working environment? Why or why not?

2. Do you think the virtual office is a good idea? Why or why not?

3. Pamela Kruger says that where employees were once willing to sacrifice evenings and weekends for their company, they are now looking at quality of life issues. What does she mean by this statement?

READING TWO

➤BEFORE YOU BEGIN

Often we build long-lasting relationships with the people we work with. The trust and support we develop for one another can create a good working environment. There are situations, however, where competition at work can create difficulties. One person may take advantage of another in order to get ahead. Sometimes people just want to make life difficult for other people at work. The story you are going to read illustrates just how difficult relationships related to work can be. Do you know of anyone (maybe yourself) who has had a difficult time at work? Sit with a partner and explain this situation.

➤READING SKILL PRACTICE: Inferences from Pictures

Look at the picture that accompanies Reading Two. What exactly do you see? List three or four important details.

a._____

b._____

c._____

d._____

2. Consider the message implied by the information in the picture. What inference can you make based on the clues in the picture? Explain.

_____

_____

3. Share your inferences with a partner. Note: Your inferences may differ based on your background knowledge and experience.

4. Finally, use the inferences you made about the picture to help you guess what Reading Two will be about. Check the statement below that best matches your guess.

This reading will be about:

a. _____ a holiday

b. _____ life and work

c. _____ culture and traditions

➤ AS YOU READ

Read the short story "A Handful of Dates" once, quickly, without your dictionary. Use these questions to help you understand the story as you read.

1. *Who* is the main character?

2. *Where* does the story take place?

3. *When* does the story take place?

4. *What* happens?

A HANDFUL OF DATES
by Taieb Saleh

1 I must have been very young at the time. While I don't remember exactly how old I was, I do remember that when people saw me with my grandfather they would pat me on the head and give my cheek a pinch—things they didn't do to my grandfather. The strange thing was that I never used to go out with my father, rather it was my grandfather who would take me with him wherever he went, except for the mornings when I would go to the mosque[1] to learn the Koran[2]. The mosque, the river and the fields—these were the landmarks in our life. While most of the children of my age grumbled at having to go to the mosque to learn the Koran, I used to love it. The reason was, no doubt, that I was quick at learning by heart and the Sheikh[3] always asked me to stand up and recite the *Chapter of the Merciful* whenever we had visitors, who would pat me on my head and cheek just as people did when they saw me with my grandfather.

2 Yes, I used to love the mosque, and I loved the river too. When we finished our Koran reading in the morning I would throw down my wooden slate and dart off[4], quick as a genie, to my mother, hurriedly swallow my breakfast, and run off for a plunge in the river. When tired of swimming about I would sit on the bank and gaze at the strip of acacia trees. I loved to give rein to my imagination and picture to myself a tribe of giants living behind the trees, a people tall and thin with white beards and sharp noses, like my grandfather. Before my grandfather ever replied to my many questions he would rub the tip of his nose with his forefinger: as for his beard, it was soft

---

[1] *mosque:* a building in which Muslims worship
[2] *Koran:* the holy book of Muslims
[3] *Sheikh:* an Arab chief or ruler
[4] *dart off:* run away suddenly

and luxuriant and as white as cotton—never in my life have I seen anything of purer whiteness or greater beauty. My grandfather must have also been extremely tall, for I never saw anyone in the whole area address him without having to look up at him, nor did I see him enter a house without having to bend so low that I was put in mind of the way the river wound round behind the acacia trees. I loved him and would imagine myself, when I grew to be a man, tall and slender like him, walking along with great stories.

3   I believe I was his favorite grandchild: no wonder, for my cousins were a stupid bunch and I—so they say—was an intelligent child. I used to know when my grandfather wanted me to laugh, when to be silent; also I would remember the times for his prayers and would bring him his prayer-rug and fill the ewer[5] for his ablutions[6] without his having to ask me. When he had nothing else to do he enjoyed listening to me reciting to him from the Koran in a lilting voice, and I could tell from his face that he was moved.

4   One day I asked him about our neighbor Masood. I said to my grandfather: 'I fancy you don't like your neighbor Masood?'

5   To which he answered, having rubbed the tip of his nose: 'He's an indolent man and I don't like such people.'

6   I said to him: 'What's an indolent man?'

7   My grandfather lowered his head for a moment, then looking across at the wide expanse of field, he said: 'Do you see it stretching out from the edge of the desert up to the Nile band? A hundred feddans. Do you see all those date palms? And those trees—*sant*, acacia, and *sayal*? All this fell into Masood's lap, was inherited by him from his father.'

8   Taking advantage of the silence that had descended upon my grandfather, I turned my gaze from him to the vast area defined by his words. 'I don't care,' I told myself, 'who owns those date palms, those trees, or this black, cracked earth—all I know is that it's the arena for my dreams and my playground.'

9   My grandfather then continued: 'Yes, my boy, forty years ago all this belonged to Masood—two-thirds of it is now mine.'

10   This was news to me, for I had imagined that the land had belonged to my grandfather ever since God's Creation.

---

[5] *ewer*: a large container for liquids
[6] *ablutions*: washing parts of one's body, in this case, before praying

11   'I didn't own a single feddan when I first set foot in this village. Masood was then the owner of all these riches. The position has   70 changed now, though, and I think that before Allah[7] calls me to Him I shall have bought the remaining third as well.'

12   I do not know why it was I felt fear at my grandfather's words— and pity for our neighbor Masood. How I wished my grandfather wouldn't do what he said! I remembered Masood's singing, his   75 beautiful voice and powerful laugh that resembled the gurgling of water. My grandfather never used to laugh.

13   I asked my grandfather why Masood had sold his land.

14   'Women,' and from the way my grandfather pronounced the word I felt that 'women' was something terrible. 'Masood, my boy, was a   80 much-married man. Each time he married he sold me a feddan or two.' I made the quick calculation that Masood must have married some ninety women. Then I remembered his three wives, his shabby appearance, his lame donkey and its dilapidated[8] saddle, his *galabia*[9] with the torn sleeves. I had all but rid my mind of the thoughts that   85 jostled in it when I saw the man approaching us, and my grandfather and I exchanged glances.

15   'We'll be harvesting the dates today,' said Masood. 'Don't you want to be there?'

16   I felt, though, that he did not really want my grandfather to   90 attend. My grandfather, however, jumped to his feet and I saw that his eyes sparkled momentarily with an intense brightness. He pulled me by the hand and we went off to the harvesting of Masood's dates.

17   Someone brought my grandfather a stool covered with an ox-hide, while I remained standing. There was a vast number of people there,   95 but though I knew them all, I found myself for some reason watching Masood: aloof from that great gathering of people, he stood as though it were no concern of his, despite the fact that the date palms to be harvested were his own. Sometimes his attention would be caught by the sound of a huge clump of dates crashing down from   100 on high. Once he shouted up at the boy perched on the very summit of the date palm who had begin hacking at a clump with his long, sharp sickle: 'Be careful you don't cut the heart of the palm.'

---

[7] *Allah:* the Muslim name for God
[8] *dilapidated:* broken down and fallen to pieces
[9] *galabia:* a long loose type of robe worn by men in many Arab countries. It is full and loose to keep the body cool and protect against the sun

18   No one paid any attention to what he said and the boy seated at the very summit of the date palm continued, quickly and energetically, to work away at the branch with his sickle till the clump of dates began to drop like something descending from the heavens. 105

19   I, however, had begun to think about Masood's phrase 'the heart of the palm.' I pictured the palm tree as something with feeling, something possessed of a heart that throbbed. I remembered Masood's remark to me when he had once seen me playing about with the branch of a young palm tree: 'Palm trees, my boy, like humans, experience joy and suffering.' And I felt an inward and unreasoned embarrassment. 110

20   When I again looked at the expanse of ground stretching before me I saw my young companions swarming like ants around the trunks of the palm trees, gathering up dates and eating most of them. The dates were collected into high mounds. I saw people coming along and weighing them into measuring bins and pouring them into sacks, of which I counted thirty. The crowd of people broke up, except for Hussein the merchant, Mousa the owner of the field next to ours on the east, and two men I'd never seen before. 115 120

21   I heard a low whistling sound and saw that my grandfather had fallen asleep. Then I noticed that Masood had not changed his stance, except that he had placed a stalk in his mouth and was munching at it like someone surfeited[10] with food that doesn't know what to do with the mouthful he still has. 125

22   Suddenly my grandfather woke up, jumped to his feet and walked towards the sacks of dates. He was followed by Hussein the merchant, Mousa the owner of the field next to ours, and the two strangers. I glanced at Masood and saw that he was making his way towards us with extreme slowness, like a man who wants to retreat but whose feet insist on going forward. They formed a circle round the sacks of dates and began examining them, some taking a date or two to eat. My grandfather gave me a fistful, which I began munching. I saw Masood filling the palms of both hands with dates and bringing them up close to his nose, then returning them. 130 135

23   Then I saw them dividing up the sacks between them. Hussein the merchant took ten; each of the strangers took five. Mousa the owner of the field next to ours on the eastern side took five, and my 140

_____

[10] *surfeited*: filled too full

grandfather took five. Understanding nothing, I looked at Masood and saw that his eyes were darting about to left and right like two mice that have lost their way home.

24   'You're still fifty pounds in debt to me,' said my grandfather to Masood. 'We'll talk about it later.'   145

25   Hussein called his assistants and they brought along donkeys, the two strangers produced camels, and the sacks of dates were loaded on to them. One of the donkeys let out a braying which set the camels frothing at the mouth and complaining noisily. I felt myself drawing close to Masood, felt my hand stretch out towards him as   150 though I wanted to touch the hem of his garment. I heard him make a noise in his throat like the rasping of a lamb being slaughtered. For some unknown reason, I experienced a sharp sensation of pain in my chest.

26   I ran off into the distance. Hearing my grandfather call after me,   155 I hesitated a little, then continued on my way. Quickening my pace, it was as though I carried within me a secret I wanted to rid myself of. I reached the riverbank near the bend it made behind the acacia trees. Then, without knowing why, I put my finger into my throat and spewed up the dates I'd eaten.   160

➤ GETTING THE MAIN IDEAS

Complete this summary of the main ideas with words from the list.

indolent   none   grandfather   sick   land   aloof

The _____ wants to own all Masood's _____ and tells his
          (1)   (2)
grandson that Masood is _____. Masood is _____ from the
                              (3)   (4)
rest of the men at the date harvest and afterwards the men take the sacks of
dates leaving Masood with _____. The boy feels _____ for
                                (5)   (6)
some reason after spending the day with his grandfather.

➤ VOCABULARY IN CONTEXT

Find each word in the paragraph indicated in brackets [ ]. Use context clues to determine the meaning of the word. Then circle the best definition.

1. recite [1]
   a. say from memory
   b. talk about

2. rein [2]
   a. control
   b. freedom

3. lilting [3]
   a. angry
   b. rising and falling

4. indolent [5]
   a. lazy
   b. successful

5. pity [12]
   a. to feel sorry for
   b. to be afraid of

6. shabby [14]
   a. expensive
   b. old and worn

7. aloof [17]
   a. separate
   b. happy with

➤ **TAKING A CLOSER LOOK**

Read the story again more carefully, still without using your dictionary. Now check your understanding of the story by filling in the information in the following story map. When you finish discuss your answers with your classmates.

1. The main character is _____.

    a. Masood, the owner of the date palms

    b. The young boy, the narrator, who has come to visit his grandfather

    c. The grandfather who lives near Masood

2. The story takes place in _____.

    a. a mosque in a small village just at sunset

    b. the grandfather's house in the morning after prayers

    c. in Masood's field of date palms during the day

3. The grandfather thinks Masood is a _____.

    a. lazy man

    b. happy man

    c. hard-working man

4. All Masood's land will someday belong to _____.

    a. the grandfather because Masood needs more money

    b. the boy because his grandfather will give it to him

    c. Mousa because he wants more date palms

5. During the date harvest the boy notices how_____.

    a. sad his grandfather looks when he sees the dates palms

    b. Masood seems to keep a distance from the other men

    c. difficult it is to harvest dates

6. The sacks of dates were _____.

    a. divided up equally among Masood and all the other men

    b. sold by Masood to all the men in the field

    c. taken by all the men except Masood

7. At the end of the date harvest the boy _____.

    a. shakes hands with Masood

    b. quickly helps his grandfather on his way

    c. feels sick and tries to get away quickly

➤ READING SKILL: Making Inferences from Fiction

By noticing clues we can infer unstated meanings from fiction. The details of a setting, the appearance of a character, and what a character says and does are important clues to base our inferences on.

➤ READING SKILL PRACTICE: Making Inferences from Fiction

- What can you infer from the short story "A Handful of Dates?"

- Read the questions and possible inferences (*a, b, c*) below.

- Read the paragraph(s).

- Mark *a, b,* and *c*:

    CI (correct inference)

    NC (not a correct inference)

    MI (need more information)

- Underline the information in the paragraph(s) that helped you make the correct inference.

Example:

What can we infer about the grandfather and Masood from paragraph 12?

    a. _NC_ the grandfather feels sorry for Masood

    b. _CI_ Masood used to be happy and the grandfather was unhappy

    c. _MI_ Masood doesn't laugh anymore

Underlined in paragraph 12: <u>Masood's powerful laugh, My grandfather never used to laugh.</u>

1. What can we infer from the description of the grandfather in paragraph 2?

    a. _____ He must have been a very old man at the time.

    b. _____ He must have been very rich at the time.

    c. _____ He must have been a very distinguished-looking man.

2. What can we infer about the grandfather's character from paragraphs 9 & 11?

    a. _____ He is a deeply religious man.

    b. _____ He is an ambitious man.

    c. _____ He is willing to help others.

3. What can we infer about Masood's financial situation from paragraph 14?

    a. _____ He has very little money these days.

    b. _____ His land is worth a lot of money if he wants to sell it.

    c. _____ He has given all his money to his wives.

4. What can we infer about Masood from his remarks in paragraph 19?

    a. _____ He knows a lot about growing dates.

    b. _____ He is a sensitive human being.

    c. _____ He doesn't really care about the palm trees.

5. From Masood's actions in paragraph 22, how do you think he feels?

    a. _____ He is upset because the men are eating his dates.

    b. _____ He feels helpless because the men have control over his date harvest.

    c. _____ He is not happy with the quality of the dates.

6. What can we conclude from the boy's action in paragraph 26?

    a. _____ He ate too many dates.

    b. _____ He is angry with his grandfather.

    c. _____ He is upset because Masood was treated inhumanly.

➤ COMMUNICATE

How important is work to you? How important are family and personal relationships?

1. Read the following and mark each one:

    I = important to me

    NI = not important to me

    _____ spending time with family and friends

    _____ gaining status at work

    _____ earning money for my future goals

    _____ developing good relationships with colleagues (the people you work with)

    _____ working overtime to show that I am dedicated to my job

    _____ earning money to support my family

    _____ having personal interests outside of work

    _____ developing expertise in the work I do

    _____ contributing to society by doing my job

    _____ respecting the rights of others both at home and in the workplace.

2. When you finish, get together with a partner and compare your choices. Give reasons for each choice.

Use the expressions from the Appendix on pages 211-214 to help you.

➤ INTERACTIVE JOURNAL RESPONSE

Choose one of the following questions and write a response. Be prepared to give an oral summary.

1. What can you infer from the title "A Handful of Dates?"

2. At the beginning of the story (paragraph 2), the narrator tells us how much he admires his grandfather as a young boy. What is his opinion at the end of the story? Find evidence in the story to support your answer.

3. What do you think about the grandfather's business relationship with Masood? Do you think he was fair in his business dealings with Masood, or do you feel he took advantage of Masood's situation? Support your opinion.

4. Consider the story in terms of work. What kind of work has led to the grandfather's wealth and power? Masood had been wealthy—how has he lost his wealth? What is Masood's view of his work with the date trees? What is the grandfather's philosophy of work? Whose view of work do you agree with more?

INEQUALITY

Despite diversity and location, there is a striking commonality of experience across countries, cultures, rural and urban areas, and age and gender divides for the poor. It can be described as a state of powerlessness: the inability to control one's life, the lack of freedom of choice and action resulting from the gap that exists between the rich and the poor.

READING ONE

► BEFORE YOU BEGIN

Inequality is the difference in social status, wealth, opportunity, rights and responsibilities, between two or more people or groups in a society. While some claim global integration and the march of technological progress will give everyone a fair and equal chance in life, others fear it will benefit only a few, creating more inequality in the world. What do you think? Read these statements about inequality and decide whether they are true (T) or false (F). You can check to see if your answers are correct after reading "Inequality in the World."

1. _____ Only people in developing countries need worry about inequality.

2. _____ Information technology can play an important role in reducing the level of inequality both within and between countries.

3. _____ Global integration will benefit only the wealthy creating greater inequality in the world.

4. _____ Education is the best way to overcome inequality.

► AS YOU READ

Skim "Inequality in the World" to get an idea of what it is about. When you finish go back and check your answers in *Before You Begin*.

INEQUALITY IN THE WORLD
by Nancy Birdsall, from *Foreign Policy*

1   Ironically, inequality is growing at a time when the triumph of the technological revolution and open markets was supposed to usher in a new age of freedom and opportunity.

The facts

2   In the United States, where the impact of global integration and the information revolution is probably the most widespread, the facts are sobering. Income inequality there is increasing, not only because of gains at the top, but more disturbingly, because of losses at the bottom. The average wage of white male high-school graduates

fell 15 percent from 1973 to 1993, and the number of men aged 25 to 54 years earning less than $10,000 a year grew. Possibly for the first time in the nation's history, educational gains may be reinforcing rather than offsetting[1] income inequality: Higher education has become a prerequisite for economic success, but because access to it can depend on family income, the poor are at a distinct disadvantage. [10]

3   Elsewhere, the forces of change—whether the spread of capitalism[2] and global integrations, or simply the march of technological progress—have at best reinforced, or at worst, made the situation even more grim. In Latin America, the ratio of income of the top 20 percent of earners to the bottom is about 16 to 1, compared with about 10 to 1 in the United States and about 5 to 1 in Western Europe. The wage gap between the skilled and the unskilled increased by more than 30 percent in Peru, 20 percent in Colombia, and nearly 25 percent in Mexico during the 1990s. Ironically, these were the countries with the greatest wage increases. [15][20]

4   The situation is less clear but no more heartening in other parts of the world. In China, the liberalization of agriculture and other market reforms has stimulated growth, yet large segments of the population have been left behind. In the affluent countries of northern Europe, increases in poor immigrant populations, growing unemployment, and economic restrictions are undermining the historic commitment of these nations to address inequality. Economic growth (or in some countries lack of growth) has seemed everywhere to be accompanied by persistent, often high, and sometimes worsening, inequality within countries. [25][30]

Causes of inequality

5   Inequality is nobody's fault and cannot be fixed in our lifetime. Understanding its causes, however, can help determine what can be done about it and what might actually make it worse. [35]

6   Inequality often creates more inequality. Therefore, history matters. Consider Latin America. The combination of mineral wealth, soils, and climate suitable for sugar production, and imported slave labor, or conquered indigenous[3] labor, helped produce two castes: large [40]

---

[1] *offsetting:* a situation where two things balance out
[2] *capitalism:* an economic and political system in which property, business, and industry are privately owned, giving individuals an opportunity to make a profit instead of the state
[3] *indigenous:* native to a country

landowners and politically unarmed workers. In 1950, just 1.5 percent of farm owners in Latin America accounted for ownership of 65 percent of all agricultural land; unequal land distribution, then the highest in the world, has risen since. Wealth in land and natural resources has invited concentration of incomes and created inequality throughout history.

7   Another source of some inequality lies in predictable human behavior. Because the rich and educated marry each other, as do the poor and uneducated, family income gaps widen. In many countries, the poor are members of ethnic or racial groups. They often suffer discrimination in the labor market, resulting in low pay and low job status.

8   The same happens with fertility. The poor and the less educated tend to have more children. As is to be expected, spending per child on nutrition, health, and education declines with the number of children. Less spending on children perpetuates the cycle of poverty and inequality.

9   Prosperity can produce inequality—an outcome that, within limits, may be economically justifiable. After all, some inequality may encourage innovation and hard work. However, with the introduction of capitalism, the newfound inequality in China and in Eastern Europe may simply mean that new economic incentives are creating opportunities for only some individuals to excel and profit.

10   Technology plays a central role in the drama of inequality. While some claim the technological revolution promises to build a global society in which no one is left out, others fear it could create more poverty and inequality, the dilemma being that this very technology will create a "digital divide" between countries that have access to technology and those that do not. We have yet to see how this will play out.

11   The most avoidable and thus most disappointing source of inequality is government policies that restrict economic growth and fuel inflation—the most devastating outcome of all for the poor. Most populist programs designed to attract the support of the working class hurt workers in the long run. When financed by unsustainable fiscal largesse[4], they bring inflation and high interest rates, which in turn hurts the poor even more.

---

[4] *fiscal largesse*: government spending; in this case, to benefit workers and the poor

12   Bad policy also includes what governments fail to do. Failure to invest in the education and skills of the poor is a fundamental cause   80
of inequality. When adequate education does not reach enough of any population, educated workers become scarce, and employers compete for them by offering higher wages. The widening wage gap between college graduates and others in many regions of the world indicates that the demand for graduates still exceeds the supply,   85
feeding inequality.

Bringing about equality

13   Economic growth that is based on the intensive use of labor reduces income inequality—within as well as across countries. One way to create equality is to build on worker-based growth. The reliance on people, technology and skills can lead to both equitable   90
growth and reduced income gaps.

14   In the increasingly service-oriented global economy, education and skills represent a kind of wealth. They are key assets and once acquired cannot be taken away, even from those who are otherwise powerless. Moreover, as education is shared more broadly, other   95
assets such as land, stocks, or money will become less important. But without a jump-start[5] from public policy, the rich will become educated and stay rich, and the poor will not, perpetuating the inequality of assets and income across generations. In the United States, Europe, and in today's poor developing countries, the single   100
best weapon against income inequality is education.

15   Relatively low levels of income inequality in China, Cuba, and the former Soviet Union seem to suggest that authoritarian politics can at least produce equality. But in fact, it is the democracies that have over time generated sustained and equalizing economic growth, and   105
have created opportunities and incentives for the poor to improve their lives. In today's global market, democracy is a key factor in realizing equality.

16   Perhaps the best way to bring about equality is to provide opportunities for the poor. This does not mean directly providing   110
services, but giving tax breaks, providing micro-loans—very small loans—to the poor, and most important of all respecting the Universal Declaration on Human Rights, which asserts the right to a

---

[5] *jump-start:* help at the beginning

standard of living adequate for the health and well-being of each and
every family.   115

17   History tells us that any hopes for a quick fix for inequality are
misplaced. During a long transition from agriculture to industry,
changes in production and in the structure of employment caused
wrenching inequality. Much inequality today may be the natural
outcome of what is a similar transition from an industrial to an   120
information age, but if it is acted upon it can be overcome. It is
important to remember that inequality is not created by the poor but
by the institutions and policies that the "better off" have established.

➤ GETTING THE MAIN IDEA

Complete this summary of the main ideas with words from the list.

working class   technological revolution

education   inequality   wage gap   income

According to the author of this article, _____ is becoming widespread
                                              (1)
in the world because of the _____ and the open market system.
                                  (2)
Government policies designed to benefit the wealthy widen the _____
                                                                    (3)
and hurt the _____. The author believes that _____ is the
                  (4)   (5)
best weapon against _____ inequality.
                          (6)

➤ VOCABULARY IN CONTEXT

Find each word in the reading (the paragraph is in brackets [ ]). Use context
clues to guess the meaning of the word. Circle a or b.

1. triumph [1]
   a. failure
   b. success

2. impact [2]
   a. effect
   b. need

3. grim [3]

   a. good

   b. bad

4. stimulated [4]

   a. caused

   b. prevented

5. persistent [4]

   a. continuing

   b. not serious

6. perpetuates [8]

   a. continues

   b. changes

7. prosperity [9]

   a. no change

   b. good times, economically

8. scarce [12]

   a. there are not enough

   b. there are too many

➤ TAKING A CLOSER LOOK

Part A: The Details

Read "Inequality in the World" again, focusing on details. Choose a or b to complete the statements. When you finish, compare your answers with your classmates' answers.

1. In the United States, economic success is dependent on _____.

   a. the technological revolution

   b. higher education

2. The largest wage gap between the skilled and unskilled during the 1990s occured in _____.

   a. Peru

   b. Mexico

3. One reason for inequality in Latin America is the _____.

   a. history of unequal land distribution

   b. history of unemployment

4. According to the author, the poor and less educated tend to have _____.

   a. larger families

   b. smaller families

5. Market reforms have _____ Chinese citizens.

   a. created economic opportunities for all

   b. only helped a small proportion of

6. The wage gap widens as the _____.

   a. number of college graduates increases

   b. number of college graduates decreases

Part B: Making Inferences

Make inferences to answer these questions.

1. Who may suffer from the digital divide? (paragraph 10)

2. What can you infer about the author's position on government policies from paragraphs 11 and 12?

3. Does the author think the poor are benefiting from government policies in China and Cuba? What evidence do you have to support your answer? (paragraph 15)

4. Do you think the author believes inequality can be overcome? What supports your answer?

➤ READING SKILL: Text Mapping (1)

Text mapping is a method of note taking that helps you condense a reading passage into a simplified format. It is especially useful when you need to read and remember the main ideas from long or difficult reading passages. A text map also serves as a useful study guide when preparing for a test. Many essays and longer reading passages are already divided into sections with subheadings which make mapping easier.

➤ READING SKILL PRACTICE: Text Mapping (1)

Part A

As you noticed, Reading One is divided into sections with subheadings. Study this text map of Reading One.

Topic: Inequality in the World

The Facts

Income inequality is increasing in many regions of the world because of:

- the technological revolution
- open markets
- global integration

Causes of Inequality

- history of land ownership and control over natural resources
- human behavior repeats itself
- prosperity through new incentives helps only a few people
- technology creates a dilemma—digital divide/global society
- bad policies widen the gap between the rich and poor

Bringing about Equality

> - worker-based growth—reliance on people, technology and skills
> - democracy improves the lives of the poor
> - education and skill training are key factors
> - opportunities such as tax breaks, micro-loans

Part B

Use the text map to answer these questions.

1. What is the topic of the reading? _____

2. How many sections does the reading have? _____

3. Name each section: _____

4. If you were reviewing for a test, under which subheading would you look for the following information?

   a. The problem of unequal land distribution: _____

   b. Details about income inequality in the world: _____

   c. The importance of education in advancing the lives of the poor:

   _____

   d. The main reasons for income inequality in the world today:

   _____

➤ INTERACTIVE JOURNAL RESPONSE

Choose one of the following questions and write a response. Be prepared to give an oral summary.

1. What do you consider to be the cause(s) of inequality in your country? Explain.

2. The technological revolution is seen by some as the best way to achieve equality on a global scale. Others, however, claim it has made the situation worse by creating a digital divide. What is your opinion? Whose responsibility is it to ensure that all nations can benefit equally from digital technology?

3. Many countries claim to support social programs (housing subsidies, school vouchers, equal employment opportunities, etc.) aimed at helping the poor. In reality, however, often the poor do not have access to information, services and resources to benefit from them. Investigate the social programs that are available in your country. Do you think the poor are benefiting from them? Why or why not? Report on your findings.

READING TWO

➤ BEFORE YOU BEGIN

1. Look at the photograph, read the title, and skim the first paragraph of Reading Two. What inference can you make?

    a. _____ The women in the picture are not poor. They live comfortable lives.

    b. _____ The women in the picture are poor.

2. Skim the last paragraph of the reading. Do you think you were you right in your answer to question 1, or do you need to change your answer?

➤ AS YOU READ

Skim the rest of "Poorest Women Gaining Equality" to get an idea of what it is about.

POOREST WOMEN GAINING EQUALITY
by Betsy Brill, from *The Examiner*

1   Bangladesh— Wrapped in bright fabric and carrying worn pink bankbooks, women arrive alone and in pairs. They slip through the sides of a tin-roofed bamboo shelter and drop to the woven mats covering the smooth

earthen floor. Squatting or folding their legs under their thin bodies, the women arrange themselves in eight neat rows. Many carefully count out piles of money they then pass to the woman at the end. As each row fills with five women, a young man on a black bicycle pedals up. The chattering women clamber to their feet and, standing tall and smiling brightly, raise their hands to greet him. He sits on a bench in front while they arrange themselves on the mats. The Grameen Bank is open.

2   The Grameen Bank, founded by Muhammed Yunus, is one of the world's first institutions to make micro-loans—very small loans—to the poor. Others have followed and discovered the same thing—not only do poor people repay their debts, but business credit helps fight poverty and inequality. The lives of 8 million to 10 million people worldwide are being lifted out of poverty through access to credit.

History of Grameen Bank

3   From a desire to learn about the real economics of the poor, Yunus, a former economics professor at Chittagong University in Bangladesh, started a research project with his students in 1976. Because Chittagong University is located in a rural area, it was easy for him to visit impoverished households in the neighboring village of Jobra. Over the course of many visits, he learned all about the lives of the poor, and much about economics that is never taught in the classroom. From his work with the poor he made some very simple conclusions. "Poor people need credit, not charity. They need what every rich business owner needs to get richer: credit and capital to build businesses and incomes."

4   His research revealed that frequently the villagers needed less than a dollar a person but could get that money only by selling their goods to moneylenders, who then lent money at very high fixed prices. Witnessing this daily tragedy moved him to action. With the help of his graduate students, he made a list of those who needed small amounts of money. They came up with 42 people. The total amount they needed was $27. From his own pocket, he lent $27 to those on his list.

5   Realizing there were many others who could benefit from access to credit, he decided to approach the university's bank and try to persuade

it to lend to the local poor. The manager would have nothing to do with his idea. Refusing to give up, he continued to meet with higher officials at local banks to ask for loans for the needy. The officials, however, also turned him down: the villagers, they argued, were not creditworthy. After some deliberation, Yunus offered himself as a guarantor to get the loans, and in 1976 he took a loan from the local bank and distributed the money to poverty-stricken individuals in Jobra. Without exception, the villagers paid back their loans. Confronted with this evidence, the bank still refused to grant them loans directly, and so he did the same thing in another village, and again it was successful. He kept expanding his work, from two to five, to 20, to 50, to 100 villages, all to convince the bankers that they should be lending to the poor. Since the bankers would not change their view of those who had no collateral[1], he decided to create a separate bank for the impoverished. After a great deal of work and negotiation with the government, the Grameen Bank ("village bank" in Bengali) was established in 1983.

Micro-loan system

6   From the outset, the Grameen Bank was built on principles that ran counter to the conventional wisdom of banking. It sought out the very poorest borrowers, and required no collateral. At first, Yunus offered loans to men because they, typically, were the bread-winners. But men frequently would gamble or drink away the money, he learned. Women turned out to be far more reliable borrowers and, unlike their husbands, they invested their money in food, clothing, and education for their children. Across cultural and geographic boundaries, these facts have held true, and most micro-lending organizations now target women.

7   The women are required to join the bank in self-formed groups of five, electing a leader and a secretary. They spend a week memorizing the bank's rules and its "Sixteen Decisions," a social contract in which, among other things, borrowers agree to drink only water that is boiled or pumped from a safe source, to limit the size of their families, to educate their children, to grow vegetables, to refuse to give or receive dowry—the money or goods a bride's family pays to the family to the groom upon marriage.

---

[1] *collateral:* money or land used as a guarantee that a loan will be paid back

8   Group members decide among themselves which two will receive the first loans—usually the neediest. The bank does not wait for borrowers to come to the bank; it brings the bank to the people. Loan payments are made in weekly meetings of six to eight groups, held in the villages where the members live. When the first two have made payments for five weeks, the following two receive their loans, and make five payments. Then the final borrower receives her loan. Initial loans average 3,000 taka ($65). 85

9   Subsequent loans grow increasingly larger, and a missed installment stains not just the borrower's record, but those of her group members, as well. No one can receive a larger loan if one person is in default. In 38,766 villages every week, 2.3 million people—most of them women, all of them poor—repeat this ritual. Without 1 taka (2 cents) of collateral, these unusual borrowers boast repayment rates exceeding 95 percent. 90 95

10   Beyond borrowers' remarkable repayment rates is their success in boosting their families' incomes. A World Bank study concluded that the Grameen Bank "alleviates poverty on a sustainable basis and makes a net contribution to local economic growth." Another study found that more than half of 10-year borrowers were leaving poverty. 100

11   Today, the Grameen Bank is an independent financial institution that has lent more than $2 billion, upward of $40 million a month in 1997. After years of reliance on donor money, the bank supports itself with interest from its loans.

Micro-loans worldwide

12   The Grameen model has now been applied in 40 countries. The first replication[2], begun in Malaysia in 1986, currently serves 40,000 poor families; their repayment rate has consistently stayed near 100 percent. In Bolivia, micro-credit has allowed women to make the transition from "food for work" programs to managing their own businesses. Within two years the majority of women in the program acquire enough credit history and financial skills to qualify for loans from mainstream[3] banks. Similar success stories are coming in from programs in poor countries everywhere. These banks all target the most impoverished, lend to groups and usually lend primarily to women. 105 110 115

---

[2] *replication:* copy
[3] *mainstream:* ordinary, regular

13   The Grameen Bank in Bangladesh has been economically self-sufficient since 1995. Similar institutions in other countries are slowly making their way toward self-reliance. A few small programs are also running in the U.S., such as inner city Chicago. Unfortunately, because labor costs are much higher in the U.S. than in developing countries—which often have a large pool[4] of educated unemployed who can serve as managers or accountants – the operations are more expensive there. As a result, the U.S. programs have had to be heavily subsidized.   120

14   In all, about 22 million poor people around the world now have   125
access to small loans, and are now able to make a better life and control their own fate[5]. From what started as a small research project to learn about the poor, Yunus and his bank are now in the forefront of a world movement to provide credit to 100 million poor people by 2005. He firmly believes that eradication[6] of poverty starts   130
with people being able to control their own lives. He hopes that one day soon everyone will be able to realize his or her potential. Then, he says, "We will be able to say we are a bank of the formerly poor."

---

[4] *pool:* group
[5] *fate:* future
[6] *eradication:* to put an end to—in this case poverty

►GETTING THE MAIN IDEA

Complete this summary of the main ideas with words from the list.

women	Grameen Bank	micro-loans	
poverty	business credit	1983	Bangladesh

Muhammed Yunus founded the Grameen Bank in _____ to help
                                                                                (1)
fight _____ and inequality in _____. The bank provides
              (2)   (3)
_____ primarily to _____ to manage their own small
        (4)   (5)
businesses. The bank's system of offering _____ has proved a success;
                                                                    (6)
more than half of 10-year borrowers are no longer living in poverty. More

than 40 other countries are now using the _____ model.
                                                                    (7)

➤**VOCABULARY IN CONTEXT**

Find each word in the reading (the paragraph is in brackets [ ]). Use context clues to guess the meaning of the word. Circle *a* or *b*.

1. clamber [1]
   a. stand
   b. shout

2. deliberation [5]
   a. arguments
   b. thought

3. confronted [5]
   a. face to face
   b. impressed

4. target [6]
   a. serve
   b. avoid

5. installment [9]
   a. meeting
   b. payment

6. be in default [9]
   a. pay
   b. not pay

7. alleviates [10]
   a. reduces
   b. allows

➤ TAKING A CLOSER LOOK

Part A: The Details

Read "Poorest Women Gaining Equality" again, focusing on details. Write true (T) or false (F) for each statement. Go back to the reading and underline the sentence that supports your answer. When you finish compare your answers with your classmates' answers.

1. _____ Muhammed Yunus established the Grameen Bank in 1976.

2. _____ The first loan he offered was organized through Chittagong University.

3. _____ Grameen Bank requires collateral for all loans.

4. _____ Loans are targeted at both men and women.

5. _____ Grameen Bank makes loans to individuals as well as groups.

6. _____ Failure to pay back a loan makes it impossible to get a larger loan.

7. _____ Bangladesh's local economy is benefiting thanks to Grameen Bank.

8. _____ The Grameen micro-loan system does not exist in any other country except Bangladesh.

Part B: Making Inferences

Make inferences to answer these questions.

1. What view do you think banks in Bangladesh have of the poor? (paragraph 5)

2. After reading paragraph 13, how successful do you think the micro-credit system is in the U.S.?

3. From this reading, what is your impression of Muhammed Yunus?

➤ READING SKILL: Text mapping (2)

A reading passage with subheadings is easier to map. It is also easier to map a reading that is written in chronological order (like a timeline of events or most biographies).

Use these suggestions when mapping a reading passage:

- Survey the reading. Read the title and scan for subheadings and any other markers that divide the reading into sections.

- Map the reading in your notebook or on a separate page, using a format you can easily understand.

- Write the title and list the sections by using subheadings or key words from the reading.

- Read one section and stop. Write the main ideas of that section in your text map, then go onto the next section.

➤ READING SKILL PRACTICE: Text Mapping (2)

Below is a list of the main details in Reading Two. They are not in the right order. Write each one in the correct box in the text map. Check back to the reading to help you.

Main Details

_____ asked local banks for loans but they refused to help

_____ Yunus loaned $27 of his own money in 1976

_____ loans mostly to women

_____ no loans offered if group does not repay

_____ Yunus took a loan to offer credit to local villagers—100% payback

_____ next two in group borrow and repay

_____ Grameen Bank ("village" bank) established in 1983

_____ first two women in group borrow and repay

_____ final woman in group borrows and repays

_____ women form in groups of five

_____ goal: loans to 100 million people by 2005

_____ micro-loans now available in 40 countries

Text Map

Topic: Gramcen Bank

Introduction

History of Grameen Bank

-
-
-
-

Micro-loan system

-
-
-
-
-
-

Micro-loans worldwide

-
-

➤COMMUNICATE

The list represents some suggestions from this unit about how to reduce poverty. Prioritize the list from the most promising (1) to the least promising (9), in your opinion. When you finish, join with a partner and compare your lists. Be prepared to give reasons for your priorities.

_____ education and skill training

_____ reduce family size

_____ micro-credit

_____ charity in the form of food, clothing, and money

_____ use of technology

_____ institute land reform for equal land distribution

_____ tax breaks for the poor

_____ intensive use of labor

_____ encourage a capitalist society

Use the expressions from the Appendix on pages 211 and 212 to help you.

➤INTERACTIVE JOURNAL RESPONSE

Choose one of the following questions and write a response. Be prepared to give an oral summary.

1. How has Yunus helped to achieve equality for poor women in Bangladesh?

2. Yunus claims that poor people need credit, not charity. Do you agree? Why or why not?

3. Choose a country and research what institutions and organizations are working for the poor there. Find out what they are doing to reduce poverty. Report your findings.

WISDOM

Wisdom is something that can't be taught in school. It is passed on to us by our elders and learned slowly from our own life experience. In this unit you will read a short story and a poem about: an older person teaching a younger person. Their ways of passing on wisdom are different, but you will recognize themes of the importance of patience, beauty, courage, and pleasure.

READING ONE

➤ BEFORE YOU BEGIN

The story you are going to read was written more than 100 years ago by an American woman, and describes a culture and time quite different from the modern age. Yet the differences between the old person, Maman-Nainaine, and the young girl, Babette, are universal. Old Maman-Nainaine likes to take her time, while young Babette is quick and impatient.

Answer these questions:

1. Recall a time in childhood when you desired something very strongly. It may have been a thing, such as a toy, or an occasion, such as a school holiday. Why did you want it so badly? What did you say to your parents or do to express your frustration with waiting? How did you feel when you finally got what you wanted, or when the occasion finally arrived?

2. Sit with a partner, and interview them about their childhood memory.

➤ AS YOU READ

Read the short story "Ripe Figs" once, quickly, without your dictionary. Use these questions to help you understand the story as you read.

1. Who are the main characters?

2. Where does the story take place?

3. When does the story take place?

4. What happens?

RIPE FIGS
by Kate Chopin

1   Maman-Nainaine said that when the figs[1] were ripe Babette might go to visit her cousins down on the Bayou[2]-Lafourche[3] where the sugar cane grows. Not that the ripening of figs had the least thing to do with it, but that is the way Maman-Nainaine was.

---

[1] *fig:* a soft sweet fruit
[2] *bayou:* a wet marshy place near a river or lake
[3] *Bayou Lafourche:* a bayou area in Louisiana (US)

2   It seemed to Babette a very long time to wait; for the leaves upon   5
the trees were tender yet, and the figs were like little, green marbles.

3   But warm rains came along and plenty of strong sunshine, and
though Maman-Nainaine was as patient as the statue of la Madone[4],
and Babette as restless as a humming-bird, the first thing they both
knew it was hot summertime. Every day Babette danced out to where   10
the fig-trees were in a long line against the fence. She walked slowly
beneath them, carefully peering between the gnarled[5], spreading
branches. But each time she came disconsolate[6] away again. What
she saw there finally was something that made her sing and dance
the whole long day.   15

4   When Maman-Nainaine sat down in her stately way to breakfast,
the following morning, her muslin cap standing like an aureole[7]
about her white, placid face, Babette approached. She bore[8] a dainty porcelain platter, which she set down before her godmother[9]. It
contained a dozen purple figs, fringed around with their rich, green   20
leaves.

5   "Ah," said Maman-Nainaine arching her eyebrows, "how early
the figs have ripened this year!"

6   "Oh," said Babette, "I think they have ripened very late."

7   "Babette," continued Maman-Nainaine, as she peeled the very   25
plumpest figs with her pointed silver fruit-knife, "you will carry
my love to them all down on Bayou-Lafourche. And tell your
Tante Frosine[10] I shall look for her at Toussaint—when the
chrysanthemums[11] are in bloom."

---

[4] *la Madone:* Mary, the mother of Christ in the Christian religion
[5] *gnarled:* twisted, not smooth
[6] *disconsolate:* disappointed
[7] *aureole:* a circle of light around the head of a saint in religious paintings
[8] *bore:* carried
[9] *godmother:* a woman who acts as a sponsor or guardian of a child
[10] *Tante Frosine:* Aunt Frosine (French)
[11] *chrysanthemums:* flowers which bloom in late summer or early autumn

➤ VOCABULARY IN CONTEXT

Find each word in the reading (the paragraph is in brackets [ ]). Use context clues to guess the meaning of the word. Circle *a* or *b*.

1. ripe [1]
   a. ready to eat
   b. green

2. tender [2]
   a. old
   b. young

3. restless [3]
   a. sleepy
   b. unable to be still

4. placid [4]
   a. calm, peaceful
   b. angry, upset

5. plumpest [7]
   a. fattest
   b. hardest

➤ GETTING THE MAIN IDEAS

Complete this summary of the story with the best words from the list. You will not use all the words.

patience	easy	sold	mother
housework	difficult	ripe	cousins

This story is about a young girl, Babette, and her godmother, Maman-Nainaine.

In order to teach Babette about _____, Maman Nanaine said that
                                          (1)

she had to wait until the figs were _____ before she could visit her
                                                (2)

_____. It is _____ for Babette to wait, but eventually, the figs
        (3)   (4)

ripen and she can go.

➤TAKING A CLOSER LOOK

Part A: Details (1)

Read the story again more carefully, looking for details. Are these sentences are true (T) or false (F)? Underline a sentence or phrase which supports your answer. When you finish, compare your answers with your classmates' answers.

1. _____ The story begins in spring.

2. _____ Maman-Nainine is impatient.

3. _____ Babette disobeys her godmother.

4. _____ Babette lives with her cousins.

5. _____ When Babette sees the ripe figs, she immediately picks them and takes them to her godmother.

6. _____ Babette will visit her cousins on the Bayou-Lafourche.

Part B: Details (2)

Find four examples (phrases or words) of Babette's impatience. Then find one example of Babette's greater patience at the end of the story.

Impatience: _____ (par 2)

_____ (par 3)

_____ (par 3)

_____ (par 6)

Patience _____ (par 4)

Part C: Making Inferences

Make inferences to answer these questions:

1. Where are Babette's parents?

2. Is Maman-Nanaine rich or poor?

➤ READING SKILL: Paraphrasing

Often students are able to translate the words of a difficult reading, but are still not able to understand it. Just checking the dictionary is not enough. You need to read a difficult sentence a few times, and in your mind, replace the difficult words, phrases, and grammar with simpler ones. This process is called paraphrasing. This powerful reading strategy will help you to understand and remember what you read.

When you paraphrase, you use your own words—words you know and that are easy for you—to express the meaning of a sentence. As you read a difficult sentence, if you replace the difficult words and phrases with your own words, you are actively understanding the sentence.

There are two steps to paraphrasing:

- changing the difficult vocabulary to simple vocabulary

- changing the grammar by using your own English

Look at the following example of paraphrasing from the third paragraph of "Ripe Figs":

Original Sentence:

She walked slowly beneath them, carefully peering between the gnarled, spreading branches.

Paraphrase (same meaning, easier words and grammar):

She walked slowly under the trees. She looked carefully into the big old branches.

➤ READING SKILL PRACTICE: Paraphrasing

Part A: Paraphrasing by Replacing Difficult Words

The first step to paraphrasing is to change the difficult vocabulary to simple vocabulary. You will need to use your dictionary to find suitable words.

Look at the example again:

She walked slowly <u>beneath</u> them, carefully <u>peering</u> between the gnarled, spreading branches.

Replacing the difficult words is the first step in paraphrasing:

She walked slowly <u>under</u> them, carefully <u>looking</u> between the <u>old</u>, spreading branches.

Use your dictionary to find words or phrases you already know to replace the underlined parts of these sentences. Rewrite the sentences.

1. Original: But each time she came <u>disconsolate</u> away again.

   Paraphrase: _____

   _____

2. Original: When Maman-Nainaine sat down in her <u>stately</u> way to breakfast, her muslin cap standing like an <u>aureole</u> about her white, <u>placid</u> face, Babette <u>approached</u>.

   Paraphrase: _____

   _____

Part B: Paraphrasing by Changing Grammar

The first step to paraphrasing is choosing simple vocabulary to rewrite the sentence. But in order to be sure that you really understand the meaning, you may also need to make changes in the word order and grammar. If you can express the meaning of the original sentence in your own English (vocabulary and grammar), you almost certainly understand the meaning.

Original: *She walked slowly <u>beneath</u> them, carefully <u>peering</u> between the <u>gnarled</u>, spreading branches.*

Step One (with the difficult words replaced): *She walked slowly <u>under</u> them, carefully <u>looking</u> between the <u>old</u>, spreading branches.*

Step Two (with the grammar changed): *She walked slowly under the trees. She looked carefully into the big old branches.*

Write paraphrases of these sentences. First, replace the difficult words with easier words. Then change the grammar, expressing the original idea in your own way.

1. Original: She bore a dainty porcelain platter, which she set down before her godmother (paragraph 4)

Step One: _____

_____

Step Two: _____

_____

2. Original: It contained a dozen purple figs, fringed around with their rich, green leaves. (paragraph 4)

Step One: _____

_____

Step Two: _____

_____

➤ INTERACTIVE JOURNAL RESPONSE

Choose one of these questions and write a response. Be prepared to give an oral summary.

1. What do you think the author wanted to show us in this story? In other words, what is the theme or main idea of the story?

2. Have you ever had a lesson in patience like Babette's? Describe it.

3. If you wanted to teach a young child about patience, how would you do it?

READING TWO

➤ BEFORE YOU BEGIN

Reading Two is advice from a father to a son, written as a poem. The poet advises his son to plant vegetables between the flowers. This isn't simply gardening advice, but a symbol. Before you read the poem, discuss with a partner what you think the vegetables and flowers might symbolize.

➤ AS YOU READ

Read "Advice to My Son," paying special attention to lines 11–12 in which vegetables and flowers are mentioned. Do you have any other ideas about the meaning of these symbols after reading the poem?

ADVICE TO MY SON
by Peter Meinke

The trick is, to live your days
as if each one may be your last
(for they go fast, and young men
   lose their lives
in strange and unimaginable   5
   ways)
but at the same time, plan long
   range
(for they go slow: If you survive
the shattered[1] windshield[2] and   10
   the bursting shell[3]
you will arrive
at our approximation[4] here below
of heaven or hell).

To be specific, between the peony[5] and the rose   15
plant squash[6] and spinach, turnips and tomatoes;
beauty is nectar[7]
and nectar, in a desert, saves—
but the stomach craves stronger sustenance
than the honied[8] vine.   20
Therefore, marry a pretty girl
after seeing her mother,
speak truth to one man,
work with another;
and always serve bread with your wine.   25
But, son,
always serve wine.

---

[1] *shattered:* broken into small pieces
[2] *windshield:* the front window of a car
[3] *shell:* a metal case containing explosives
[4] *approximation:* copy
[5] *peony:* a type of flower
[6] *squash:* a type of vegetable
[7] *nectar:* a sweet refreshing drink
[8] *honied:* sweet like honey

▶VOCABULARY IN CONTEXT

Find each word in the reading (the line is in brackets [ ]). Use context clues to guess the meaning. Write your guess. Compare your answer with some of your classmates' answers. Finally, check the dictionary to see how well you guessed.

Vocabulary	Your Guess From Context	Dictionary Meaning
1. long range [6]	_____	_____
2. survive [7]	_____	_____
3. bursting [9]	_____	_____
4. craves [18]	_____	_____
5. sustenance [18]	_____	_____

▶READING SKILL: Paraphrasing Implied Meaning

As you learned, paraphrasing involves two steps: replacing difficult words, and changing the grammar. When reading poetry, paraphrasing is a very effective tool, but the reader needs to apply a third step: interpreting the implied meaning.

Poets choose words and phrases to express other levels of meaning. A flower may symbolize "beauty," while a vegetable may symbolize "necessity." So after replacing difficult vocabulary and changing the grammar, you still need to apply your imagination in order to understand the implied meaning and restate the poem in your own words. This is not easy, but it can be fun!

Original Sentence: *If you survive the shattered windshield and the bursting shell, you will arrive at our approximation here below of heaven or hell.*

Paraphrase Step One: Replacing Difficult Words

If you can live through the broken windshield and the explosions of war, you will experience our copy here below of heaven or hell.

Paraphrase Step Two: Changing Grammar

You will experience heaven on earth or hell on earth, if you can live through the broken windshield and war.

Paraphrase Step Three: Paraphrasing Implied Meaning

If you don't die in an accident or war, you will experience a happy or an unhappy life here on earth.

➤ READING SKILL PRACTICE: Paraphrasing Implied Meaning

Paraphrase these sentences from the poem by following the three steps above.

1. Beauty is nectar, and nectar in a desert saves.

   Step One: _____

   Step Two: _____

   Step Three: _____

2. But the stomach craves stronger sustenance than the honied vine.

   Step One: _____

   Step Two: _____

   Step Three: _____

➤ TAKING A CLOSER LOOK

Now that you have experience with paraphrasing, try the following exercise to check your comprehension and your paraphrasing skills. Choose the paraphrase which most closely matches the original meaning.

1. The trick is, to live your days as if each one may be the last . . . but at the same time, plan long range.

   In other words,

   a. _____ You should be tricky about living because in order to have a long life, you need to plan.

   b. _____ The important thing is to enjoy each day but also have a plan for the future.

   c. _____ It is difficult to live your last days because planning takes a long time.

2. . . . for they go fast, and young men lose their lives in strange and unimaginable ways.

In other words,

a. _____ because time goes quickly, and young men sometimes die unexpectedly.

b. _____ because young men move fast, and are confused by strange and unimaginable events.

c. _____ because young men begin to act in strange ways as they hurry through life.

3. To be specific, between the peony and the rose plant squash and spinach, turnips and tomatoes.

In other words,

a. _____ it's important to put each plant in its place.

b. _____ it's important in life to have both beautiful things and useful things.

c. _____ it's more important to pay attention to vegetables since they can be eaten.

4. Therefore, marry a pretty girl after seeing her mother.

In other words,

a. _____ before marriage, meet your girlfriend's mother since your girlfriend will probably turn out like her later in life.

b. _____ it's better to avoid trouble with mother-in-laws by marrying the daughter as soon as possible.

c. _____ after you meet her mother, you must marry the girl.

5. Always serve bread with your wine, but son, always serve wine.

In other words,

a. _____ always serve bread so you can be healthy, but always serve wine so that you can enjoy your life.

b. _____ Bread is the most important thing to serve your guests, and wine is just an extra.

c. _____ since people expect wine with their dinner, don't disappoint them by serving only bread.

► GETTING THE MAIN IDEA: Poetic Themes

Usually by skimming an article, we can find the main idea quite quickly. However, a poem requires close reading and analysis before the literary theme (main idea) becomes apparent. As you have learned, in a short story or poem, the reader has some freedom in interpreting the theme. The following is a summary of a theme of the poem. Fill in the blanks by choosing the most appropriate words from the list below. Then take a few minutes to discuss the theme with your partner. Do you agree with the poet's message? Did you notice any other themes of the poem?

practical   war   endure

worried   future   enjoy

In order to live a happy life, it is important to be _____ and plan for
                                                                (1)
the _____, but it is just as important to _____ life.
        (2)   (3)

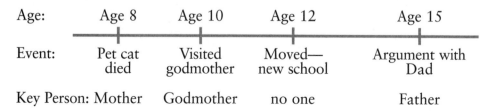

💬 ► COMMUNICATE

Time Line Discussion

A time line is a record of important events in the order in which they happened. Look at the example of a timeline below. Then make your own timeline. Choose at least three important events that have happened to you. Mention any key person who was involved with you at the time.

Example:

Age:	Age 8	Age 10	Age 12	Age 15
Event:	Pet cat died	Visited godmother	Moved— new school	Argument with Dad
Key Person:	Mother	Godmother	no one	Father

Your Time Line

Age:

Event:

Key Person:

Find a partner and ask about his or her time line. Use some of these questions to begin, and then refer to the Appendix on page 113 for more expressions for "Active Listening."

- Can you tell me about an event on your time line?

- How did you feel?

- What did you learn?

- Would you ever do that again?

➤ INTERACTIVE JOURNAL RESPONSE

Choose one of these questions and write a response. Be prepared to give an oral summary of your written response in small groups.

1. What do you think about the poet's advice in lines 20–26? Explain your response.

2. If you had/have a son or daughter, what advice would you like to give him or her?

3. Prepare a short paragraph or poem of advice. You can decide who the target of the advice will be (for example, Advice to My Daughter, Teacher, Best Friend, Boyfriend, Girlfriend, Husband, Wife, etc.). You can be serious or humorous.

CULTURE
AND CHANGE

These are exciting times for linguists and anthropologists—languages and cultures that were unknown one hundred years ago are being discovered and studied. But many of these languages are endangered. Despite efforts to protect linguistic and cultural diversity, traditions are lost. The outcome of the conflict between tradition and change in a global society remains to be seen.

READING ONE

➤ BEFORE YOU BEGIN

1. Preview the article, noticing the title, and skimming the first and last paragraphs. What does the article seem to be about?

2. There are many animals which are "endangered," that is, their numbers are so low that they may disappear altogether. Examples of endangered animals include the Chinese panda, and the Ugandan mountain gorilla. How might a language be "endangered?" Can you think of any examples?

➤ AS YOU READ

Skim "Endangered Languages" very quickly to get an idea of what it is about. Then, to prepare for this unit's reading skill of summarizing, skim the article again. Mark with your pencil any sentences or words which you think may express a main idea. Do not slow down or re-read.

ENDANGERED LANGUAGES
by David Koop, from *The Japan Times*

1   As she plays with her two laughing grandchildren, the woman with the long gray hair forgets herself in her joy and begins speaking in her native Chamicuro tongue. No one understands her. Wistfully[1], Natalia Sangama switches to Spanish—now the language of her children, her grandchildren. "I dream in Chamicuro, but I cannot tell   5 my dreams to anyone," says the last fluent speaker of the language in her village on the shore of a lake in the Amazon jungle. Four other elderly inhabitants of Pampa Hermosa, 750 km northeast of Lima, know bits and pieces of Chamicuro, but when Sangama dies, the language will die with her.   10

2   Many of the world's languages are disappearing as modern communications, migration and population growth end the isolation of ethnic groups. Linguists warn of a crash in cultural and intellectual diversity similar to what is happening in animal and plant   15 species as wilderness areas are cleared. Each language contains words that uniquely capture ideas; when the words are lost, so are the ideas.

---

[1] *wistfully:* sadly, wishing for something different

3   At least half the world's 6,000 languages will likely die out in the next century, say experts, and only 5 percent of languages are "safe," meaning they are spoken by at least a million people and receive state backing. "There are hundreds of languages that are down to a few elderly speakers and are for the most part beyond hope of revival," says Doug Whalen, a Yale University linguist who is president of the Endangered Language Fund. "It's like seeing a glacier[2]. You can tell it's coming even though it's kind of slow."   20

                                                                                                    25

4   The loss of languages is damaging because when a language dies, much of a culture dies with it, says Michael Krauss, a University of Alaska linguist who compares linguistic diversity to biological diversity. The human race evolved amid a diversity of languages, which formed a rich pool of varied ideas and world views, but the pool is shrinking fast, he says. As contact between cultures has grown with globalization, the process of dominant languages killing off smaller languages has accelerated.   30

5   The process can best be seen in places like Peru's Amazon jungle, where some languages are still being discovered while others become extinct. "South America has languages that are only now being discovered, and as soon as they are discovered they are endangered," Whalen says. Early Spanish missionaries were stunned by the number of languages they found among isolated communities separated by thick jungle. They estimated there were more than 500 languages spoken in an area half the size of Iran. Linguists now estimate there were probably 100–150 languages, but with a wide range of dialects.   35

                                                                                                    40

6   Today, only 57 survive and 25 of them are on the road to extinction, says Mary Ruth Wise, a linguist with the Dallas-based Summer Institute of Linguistics. "Language extinction begins when the children stop learning a language. Often this is motivated by shame for speaking a 'primitive' language," Wise says. "The key to preserving these languages is teaching people to hold them in esteem[3]." She points sadly to the Taushiro Indians, who live on the banks of the Aucuyacu River in Peru's jungle. About a dozen elderly tribe members are the last to speak Taushiro, one of the world's few languages with no labial[4] consonants, such as "p," "b" or "m," which require lip   45

                                                                                                    50

_____

[2] _glacier:_ a river of ice moving very slowly
[3] _esteem:_ respect
[4] _labial:_ of the lips

movement to pronounce. "They won't survive past this generation. The loss may seem trivial, but to a linguist it's a crime," Wise says.

7   In Pampa Hermosa, the last Chamicuros live without roads, electricity, or telephones. The jungle surrounds the village like a thick, green wall. But a radio blares Spanish news and salsa music from a station in Yurimaguas, a town eight hours away by river boat. Schools teach the children in Spanish, and the women have exchanged their traditional brightly colored skirts, beads and face paint for jeans and polyester dresses. Smallpox, migration, and assimilation[5] into the dominant Spanish culture have reduced the number of Chamicuros from 4,000 at the time of the Spanish conquest to 125 today. They live by fishing, hunting, and growing corn, yucca, and beans. "In the missionary school they used to make us kneel on corn if we spoke Chamicuro," Sangama recalls.

8   Farther along Lake Achual Tipishca live the Cocama-Cocamilla, a more numerous tribe of former headhunters[6] who have also lost much of their culture to the dominant Spanish-speaking mestizo[7] society. About 15,000 Cocama-Cocamilla remain, 570 in the village of Achual Tipischa, the heart of the Cocama-Cocamilla culture. Even there, only one in 10 people, all elderly, speak the tribal language. District Gov. Orlando Pereira, not one of them, recommends visitors bring liquor if they want to hear the language spoken. "They are ashamed of their language," he says. "They only speak it in front of strangers when they have been drinking." Carlos Murayari, a 64-year old river fisherman, has 11 children but none speak Cocama-Cocamilla. "I tried to teach them Cocama-Cocamilla, but Spanish took over," he says. "It's like paddling against the current."

9   Paddling against the current is hard work, and some would argue that the effort is wasted. The river of life flows in the direction of constant change, and trying to stop change is often futile. To keep endangered languages alive requires massive affirmative action, especially in this age of globalization. The establishment of government ministries, radio and TV stations, newspapers and books, cultural events, employment, even bribes might encourage a small tribe in America, Australia, or Africa to carry on using its native language.

---

[5] *assimilation*: becoming part of a group, system, or culture
[6] *headhunters*: people who collect the heads of their enemies as trophies
[7] *mestizo*: a blend of European and Native American ancestry or culture

An increasing number of scholarly organizations devoted to linguistic diversity and the preservation of minority languages (for example, the British Foundation for Endangered Languages) indicates there is   90
some academic interest, but it also requires people in top government and social services positions who are committed to preserving the endangered languages and willing to spend considerable time, energy and money to do so.

10   Should we listen to the voice that celebrates difference and aims to   95
preserve language and cultural diversity in the face of a very powerful homogenizing[8] current of change? The problem of language-extinction and even language change raises fundamental questions about value. What exactly is the value of a language? Does the existence of linguistic diversity have any value? Andrew Woodfield, Director of the   100
Centre for Theories of Language and Learning at Bristol University, warns that just as unknown but endangered plants may contain medically valuable ingredients, so unknown, endangered languages may contain hidden riches. He says "By allowing languages to die out, the human race is destroying things it doesn't understand."   105

---

[8] *homogenizing:* making separate or different things the same

➤VOCABULARY IN CONTEXT

Find each word in the reading (the paragraph is in brackets [ ]). Use context clues to guess the meaning. Write your guess. Compare your answer with some of your classmates' answers. Finally, check the dictionary to see how well you guessed.

Vocabulary	*Your Guess From Context*	*Dictionary Meaning*
1. switches to [1]		
2. backing [3]		
3. revival [3]		
4. stunned [5]		
5. trivial [6]		
6. blares [7]		

7. paddling [8]   _____   _____

8. futile [9]   _____   _____

►TAKING A CLOSER LOOK

Part A: The Details

Read "Endangered Languages" again, focusing on details. Answer the questions in your own words. When you finish, discuss the answers with your classmates.

1. Find four reasons in the article for the loss of languages.

2. Why is the disappearance of languages a bad thing, according to the article (two reasons)?

3. Approximately how many languages have disappeared from Peru's Amazon jungle?

4. What is unique about the language of Taushiro?

5. Give four examples of how Chamicuro culture has been assimilated into mestizo culture (paragraph 7).

6. What are some examples of affirmative action to keep endangered languages alive (paragraph 9)?

7. Name three endangered languages mentioned in the article.

8. Name four scholarly organizations devoted to linguistic diversity.

Part B: Making Inferences

Make inferences to answer these questions.

1. In what ways is the loss of linguistic diversity similar to the loss of biological diversity?

2. Explain Carlos Murayari's comment in paragraph 8: "It's like paddling against the current."

➤ READING SKILL: Summarizing

Summarizing is retelling the main ideas of a reading in a much shorter, simpler form. Summarizing is an excellent learning tool, because in order to express the meaning of an article in a few words, you must understand the article. Previewing, skimming, and also reading carefully for the main idea and details will help you prepare a good summary.

The length of the summary depends on the length of the original article and your instructor's expectations. A summary can be a few sentences, one short paragraph, or a few paragraphs.

➤ READING SKILL PRACTICE: Summarizing a Paragraph

Part A

A paragraph summary should be 1-2 sentences. It should express the main idea of the paragraph in a simple way. Often this is already stated by the author in the topic sentence of the paragraph. However, sometimes you will need to simplify or add to the topic sentence to make a good summary. And of course, sometimes authors do not write topic sentences. In that case, you need to skim the paragraph and decide what the main idea is.

Example: Re-read the first paragraph of "Endangered Languages" and the summary below. Notice how most of the details of the paragraph are left out of the summary. Only the most important ideas are kept in the summary.

Original paragraph: As she plays with her two laughing grandchildren, the woman with the long gray hair forgets herself in her joy and begins speaking in her native Chamicuro tongue. No one understands her. Wistfully, Natalia Sangama switches to Spanish—now the language of her children, her grand-children. "I dream in Chamicuro, but I cannot tell my dreams to anyone," says the last fluent speaker of the language in her village on the shore of a lake in the Amazon jungle. Four other elderly inhabitants of Pampa Hermosa, 750 km northeast of Lima, know bits and pieces of Chamicuro, but when Sangama dies, the language will die with her.

Summary: Natalia Sangama is the last fluent speaker of the Chamicuro language, which will disappear when she dies.

Now summarize three more paragraphs of Reading One. Write your summary (1-2 sentences) in the spaces below. When you have finished, compare your summaries with another student's.

Paragraph 3: _____

_____

Paragraph 5: _____

_____

Paragraph 7: _____

_____

➤ READING SKILL PRACTICE: Summarizing a Long Article

Part B

Summarizing a long article is more difficult than summarizing a paragraph. You need to be able to express the main idea and the important supporting ideas, in a short, simple way. One effective technique in writing a good summary is to use text mapping, as you learned in Unit 8.

Follow these steps to write a summary of "Endangered Languages."

1. Preview. Notice the title. It may express the topic or even main idea of the article. Notice any subtitles, bold headings, or italicized words. Skim the first few paragraphs and the last paragraph to see if the author gives the purpose of the article, the main idea, and the conclusions about the topic.

2. Read the article quickly all the way through. Underline the sentences or words which you think are important.

3. Read the article again more carefully. Pay more attention to the sentences you marked, making sure you grasp the main idea.

4. Ask yourself, "What does the author want to say about the topic, and what is the most important support (examples, details) for the main idea? Prepare a list of key words or phrases (your "notes"). You may want to write them in the margin, as marginal notes.

5. Arrange the main ideas and supporting details on a text map, as you learned in Unit 8.

6. From your notes and text map, write the summary. It is important that the summary is in your own words (paraphrase), is short and simple, and includes the main ideas of the article. Your summary should be about 100 words.

7. Compare your summary with another student's.

➤ GETTING THE MAIN IDEAS

"Getting the Main Ideas" should be easy after you have completed the Reading Skill Practice Exercises above! Use these key words to write a summary of the main ideas of "Endangered Languages." Write about 50 words.

endangered languages	culture	Chamicuro
6000	linguistic diversity	globalization

➤ INTERACTIVE JOURNAL RESPONSE

Choose one of these questions and write a response. Be prepared to give an oral summary.

1. In paragraph 6, Wise says about the disappearance of the Taushiro language, "The loss may seem trivial, but to a linguist it's a crime." Do you agree that it is a crime to allow languages to disappear? Explain your view.

2. How would you feel if you could never use your own native language again, and instead had to use only English to communicate with others? Are there particular social situations (for example, having an argument with your parents) in which you feel you really need your native language to truly express your thoughts and feelings? What is the value of your native language to you?

3. What would it be like if everyone in the world spoke the same language? What would be easier? Would we lose anything?

READING TWO

➤ BEFORE YOU BEGIN

Discuss these questions with a partner:

1. What were your favorite childhood games? Why?

2. What is the "generation gap"? Are there any examples from your own life when you experienced difficulty communicating with older people because of the generation gap? Tell your partner about the situation.

Read the short story "Crickets" once, quickly, without your dictionary. Use these questions to help you understand the story as you read.

1. Who are the main characters?

2. Where does the story take place?

3. What does each character want?

4. What happens?

CRICKETS

by Robert Olen Butler, from *A Good Scent from a Strange Mountain*

1   They call me Ted where I work and they've called me that for over a decade now and it still bothers me, though I'm not very happy   5 about my real name being the same as the former President of the former Republic of Vietnam. Thieu is not an uncommon name   10 in my homeland and my mother had nothing more in mind than a long-dead uncle when she gave it to me. But in Lake Charles, Louisiana, I am Ted. I guess the other Mr. Thieu[1] has enough of my former country's former gold bullion[2] tucked away so that in

---

[1] *Mr. Thieu*: Nguyen Van Thieu was the President of South Vietnam. When North Vietnam invaded South Vietnam in 1975, he escaped to Europe.

[2] *bullion*: gold or silver bars from which coins are made

London, where he probably wears a bowler[3] and carries a rolled   15
umbrella, nobody's calling him anything but Mr. Thieu.

2   I hear myself sometimes and I sound pretty bitter, I guess. But I
don't let that out at the refinery[4], where I'm the best chemical
engineer they've got and they even admit it once in a while. They're
good-hearted people, really. I've done enough fighting in my life. I   20
was eighteen when Saigon fell and I was only recently mustered into
the army[5], and when my unit dissolved and everybody ran, I stripped
off my uniform and put on my civilian clothes again and I threw
rocks at the North's tanks when they rolled through the streets. Very
few of my people did likewise. I stayed in the mouths of alleys so I   25
could run and then return and throw more rocks, but because what
I did seemed so isolated and so pathetic[6] a gesture, the gunners in the
tanks didn't even take notice. But I didn't care about their scorn. At
least my right arm had said no to them.

3   And then there were Thai Pirates in the South China Sea and idiots   30
running the refugee centers and more idiots running the agencies in
the US to find a place for me and my new bride, who braved with
me the midnight escape by boat and the terrible sea and all the rest.
We ended up here in the flat bayou[7] land of Louisiana, where there
are rice paddies and where the water and the land are in the most   35
delicate balance with each other, very much like the Mekong Delta,
where I grew up. These people who work around me are good people
and maybe they call me Ted because they want to think of me as one
of them, though sometimes it bothers me that these men are so much
bigger than me. I am the size of a woman in this country and these   40
American men are all massive and they speak so slowly, even to one
another, even though English is their native language. I've heard New
Yorkers on television and I speak as fast as they do.

4   My son is beginning to speak like the others here in Louisiana. He
is ten, the product of the first night my wife and I spent in Lake   45
Charles, in a cheap motel with the sky outside red from the refineries.
He is proud to have been born in America, and when he leaves us in
the morning to walk to the Catholic school, he says, "Have a good

---

[3] *bowler:* a type of men's hat (British)
[4] *refinery:* a factory where petroleum is refined (made into gasoline, for example)
[5] *mustered into the army:* called into army service
[6] *pathetic:* poor, useless
[7] *bayou:* a wet, marshy area

day, y'all." Sometimes I say good-bye to him in Vietnamese and he wrinkles his nose at me and says, "Aw Pop," like I'd just cracked a corny[8] joke. He doesn't speak Vietnamese at all and my wife says not to worry about that. He's an American.

5   But I do worry about that, though I understand why I should be content. I even understood ten years ago, so much so that I agreed with my wife and gave my son an American name. Bill. Bill and his father Ted. But this past summer I found my son hanging around the house bored in the middle of vacation and I was suddenly his father Thieu with a wonderful idea for him. It was an idea that had come to me in the first week of every February we'd been in Lake Charles, because that's when the crickets always begin to crow[9] here. This place is rich in crickets, which always makes me think of my own childhood in Vietnam. But I never said anything to my son until last summer.

6   I came to him after watching him slouch around the yard one Sunday pulling the Spanish moss off the lowest branches of our big oak tree and then throwing rocks against the stop sign on our corner. "Do you want to do something fun?" I said to him.

7   "Sure, Pop," he said, though there was a certain suspicion in his voice, like he didn't trust me on the subject of fun. He threw all the rocks at once that were left in his hand and the stop sign shivered at their impact.

8   I said, "If you keep that up, they will arrest me for the destruction of city property and then they will deport[10] us all."

9   My son laughed at this. I, of course, knew that he would know I was bluffing. I didn't want to be too hard on him for the boyish impulses that I myself had found to be so satisfying when I was young, especially since I was about to share something of my own childhood with him.

10   "So what've you got, Pop?" my son asked me.

11   "Fighting crickets," I said.

12   "What?"

13   Now, my son was like any of his fellow ten-year-olds, devoted to superheroes and the mighty clash of good and evil in all of its

---

[8] *corny:* silly, sentimental
[9] *crow:* a loud shrill noise (usually refers to the sound a rooster makes)
[10] *deport:* to send an unwanted person out of a country

high-tech forms in the Saturday-morning cartoons. Just to make sure he was in the right frame of mind, I explained it to him with one word, "Cricketmen," and I thought this was a pretty good ploy. He cocked his head in interest at this and I took him to the side porch and sat him down and I explained. 85

14   I told him how, when I was a boy, my friends and I would prowl the undergrowth and capture crickets and keep them in matchboxes. We would feed them leaves and bits of watermelon and bean sprouts, and we'd train them to fight by keeping them in a constant state of agitation by blowing on them and gently flicking the ends of their antennas with a sliver of wood. So each of us would have a stable of fighting crickets, and there were two kinds. 90 95

15   At this point my son was squirming a little bit and eyes were shifting away into the yard and I knew that my Cricketman trick had run its course. I fought back the urge to challenge his set of interests. Why should the stiff and foolish fights of his cartoon characters absorb him and the real clash—real life and death—that went on in the natural world bore him? But I realized that I hadn't cut to the chase[11] yet, as they say on the TV. "They fight to the death," I said with as much gravity as I could put into my voice, like I was James Earl Jones. 100

16   The announcement won me a glance and a brief lift of his eyebrows. This gave me a little scrabble of panic, because I still hadn't told him about the two types of crickets and I suddenly knew that was a real important part for me. I tried not to despair at his understanding and I put my hands on his shoulders and turned him around to face me. "Listen," I said. "You need to understand this if you are to have fighting crickets. There are two types, and all of us had some of each. One type we called the charcoal crickets. These were very large and strong, but they were slow and they could become confused. The other type was small and brown and we called them fire crickets. They weren't as strong, but they were very smart and quick." 105 110 115

17   "So who would win?" my son said.

18   "Sometimes one and sometimes the other. The fights were very long and full of hard struggle. We'd have a little tunnel made of paper and we'd slip a sliver of wood under the cowling[12] of our

---

[11] *cut to the chase:* tell your idea directly
[12] *cowling:* hard cover or shell

cricket's head to make him mad and we'd twirl him by his antenna,   120
and then we'd put our crickets into the tunnel at opposite ends.
Inside, they'd approach each other and begin to fight and then we'd
lift the paper tunnel and watch."

19   "Sounds neat," my son said, though his enthusiasm was at best
moderate, and I knew I had to act quickly.   125

20   So we got a shoe box and we started looking for crickets. It's better at night, but I knew for sure his interest wouldn't last that long.
Our house is up on blocks because of the high water table in town
and we crawled along the edge, pulling back the bigger tufts of grass
and turning over rocks. It was one of the rocks that gave us our first   130
crickets, and my son saw them and cried in my ear, "There, there,"
but he waited for me to grab them. I cupped first one and then the
other and dropped them into the shoe box and I felt a vague disappointment, not so much because it was clear that my boy did not
want to touch the insects, but that they were both the big black ones,   135
the charcoal crickets. We crawled on and we found another one in
the grass and another sitting in the muddy shadow of the house
behind the hose faucet and then we caught two more under an
azalea bush.

21   "Isn't that enough?" my son demanded. "How many do we   140
need?"

22   I sat with my back against the house and put the shoe box in my
lap and my boy sat beside me, his head stretching this way so he
could look into the box. There was no more vagueness to my feeling.
I was actually weak with disappointment because all six of these   145
were charcoal crickets, big and inert[13] and just looking around like
they didn't even know anything was wrong.

23   "Oh, no," my son said with real force, and for a second I thought
he had read my mind and shared my feeling, but I looked at him and
he was pointing at the toes of his white sneakers. "My Reeboks are   150
ruined!" he cried, and on the toe of each sneaker was a smudge of
grass.

24   I glanced back into the box and the crickets had not moved and I
looked at my son and he was still staring at his sneakers. "Listen," I
said, "this was a big mistake. You can go on and do something else."   155

---

[13] *inert*: not moving, slow to move

25   He jumped up at once. "Do you think Mom can clean these?" he said.

26   "Sure," I said. "Sure."

27   He was gone at once and the side door slammed and I put the box on the grass. But I didn't go in. I got back on my hands and knees 160 and I circled the entire house and then I turned over every stone in the yard and dug around all the trees. I found probably two dozen more crickets, but they were all the same. In Louisiana there are rice paddies and some of the bayous look like the Delta, but many of the birds are different, and why shouldn't the insects be different, too? 165 This is another country, after all. It was just funny about the fire crickets. All of us kids rooted for them, even if we were fighting with one of our own charcoal crickets. A fire cricket was a very precious and admirable thing.

28   The next morning my son stood before me as I finished my breakfast 170 and once he had my attention, he looked down at his feet, drawing my eyes down as well. "See?" he said. "Mom got them clean."

29   Then he was out the door and I called after him, "See you later, Bill."

➤ VOCABULARY IN CONTEXT

Find each word in the reading (the paragraph is in brackets [ ]). Use context clues to guess the meaning. Write your guess. Compare your answer with some of your classmates' answers. Finally, check the dictionary to see how well you guessed.

Vocabulary	Your Guess From Context	Dictionary Meaning
1. massive [3]	_____	_____
2. slouch [6]	_____	_____
3. bluffing [9]	_____	_____
4. cocked [13]	_____	_____
5. prowl [14]	_____	_____
6. agitation [14]	_____	_____
7. flicking [14]	_____	_____

8. squirming [15]   _____   _____

9. shifting [15]   _____   _____

10. a smudge [23]   _____   _____

➤GETTING THE MAIN IDEAS

In five sentences, summarize the main ideas of this story by answering these questions:

- Who are the main characters?

- Where does the story take place?

- What does the father want to do?

- Is the game of fighting crickets successful? Why or why not?

- What is the father's attitude at the end of the story?

➤TAKING A CLOSER LOOK

Part A. Details

Answer these questions.

1. Why did Ted come to the U.S.?

2. How does Louisiana compare to the Mekong Delta? That is, what are the similarities and the differences?

3. Give examples from the story to show that the son Bill follows American culture, not Vietnamese.

4. Describe the two types of crickets.

5. Describe the game of fighting crickets.

6. Why can't Bill and Ted play "fighting crickets"?

7. What is more important to Bill than the fighting crickets?

Part B: Making Inferences

Make inferences to answer these questions.

1. What kind of man is Ted? Think of several adjectives to describe him, and provide an example from the story to support each adjective.

2. What kind of boy is Bill? Think of several adjectives to describe him, and provide an example from the story to support each adjective.

3. Describe the relationship between father and son. Do they love each other or not? How do you know?

4. What do you think the crickets symbolize?

➤ READING SKILL PRACTICE: Summarizing

In 2 or 3 sentences, write a summary of the literary theme of this story, using these key words:

     family relations   generation gap   culture gap   tradition   change

➤ COMMUNICATE

Work with a partner. This activity involves two role plays: (1) a conversation between Bill and a school friend, and (2) a conversation between Ted and his wife. Do the role plays with the same partner, using the expressions for Storytelling and Active Listening that you find in the Appendix on page 213.

Read the situation and decide who will play each role. Then take about 10 minutes alone to prepare your roles. Next, do both roleplays. Finally, take a few minutes to discuss with your partner what you noticed about the differences between Bill's and Ted's points of view as they told the same story.

Directions:

Role Play One

- Student A is Bill and Student B is a school friend.

- Bill summarizes the events of the previous afternoon, when he and Ted were looking for crickets. Use the expressions for Storytelling from the Appendix on page 213 (introducing the story, showing time order, and concluding).

- Bill's friend listens actively, using the expressions for Active Listening from the Appendix on page 213 (non-verbal, short responses).

- The school friend interviews Bill, asking follow-up questions about the story and also about Bill's feelings.

Role Play Two

Student B is Ted and Student A is Ted's wife.

- Ted summarizes the events of the previous afternoon, when he and Bill were looking for crickets. Use the expressions for Storytelling from the Appendix on page 213.

- Ted's wife listens actively.

- Ted's wife interviews Ted, asking follow-up questions about the story and about Ted's feelings.

➤ INTERACTIVE JOURNAL RESPONSE

Choose one of the following questions and write a response. Be prepared to give an oral summary.

1. How does Ted change?

2. How did this story make you feel? Sad? Nostalgic? Thoughtful? Happy? Did the story remind you of an experience you have had? If so, describe it.

3. In your experience, what is the best way to manage conflict between generations (the generation gap)? How about conflicts between cultural values?

4. In the end, Ted seems to be resigned to his boy being American rather than Vietnamese. Do you think this ending is inevitable? Do you think Ted's change is appropriate?

MANAGING
NATURE

The trend of a rising population and of an increasingly industri-
alized society is taking its toll on nature. This dilemma has
generated much debate. The question remains: How can we preserve
nature while at the same time ensuring the livelihood of all human
beings?

READING ONE

➤ BEFORE YOU BEGIN

Endangered species are plants and animals that are in danger of becoming extinct if nothing is done to protect them and their habitats. The following chart gives examples of some endangered animal species in various countries. Look at the chart and answer the questions below.

Endangered	Major Threat	Conservation Actions
Mountain Gorilla (Uganda)	loss of habitat illegal hunting war	habitat protection research / eco-tourism
Giant Panda (China)	loss of habitat illegal hunting	captive breeding experimental cloning
Black Rhino (Tanzania)	loss of habitat illegal hunting	habitat protection captive breeding
Golden Lion Tamarin (Brazil)	loss of habitat illegal hunting	habitat protection captive breeding community education
Black-footed Ferret (United States)	loss of habitat illegal hunting	captive breeding community education

(Information taken from International Union for Conservation of Nature and Natural Resources / IUCN)

1. What threat do all of these endangered species have in common?

2. Which conservation measure do you think might be most effective?

➤ AS YOU READ

Skim "Protecting the Wild" to get an idea of what it is about.

Protecting the Wild

by Eric Dinerstein and Karen Baragona, from *The Washington Post*.

1   At a medical research laboratory in London, England, mice are born a quarter-century after their mothers' deaths, their embryos[1] having been preserved, frozen for future use. This technique, known as "cryopreservation," has become almost routine in genetics[2] and agriculture, as well as in the treatment of human infertility. But what about applying this miracle of mouse science and other such breakthroughs to endangered species? As habitats disappear, some scientists hope that such high-tech miracle methods will ensure the survival of endangered species, but for conservation[3] purposes, it's more a mistake than a miracle.

2   At Texas A&M University, a freezer houses canisters of eggs, sperm[4], embryos and adult cells from 18 animals threatened with extinction. This project, known as "Noah's Ark[5]" aims to preserve the lowland gorilla, the Arabian oryx, the greater kudu and other creatures by saving their genetic components while the animals still exist in their natural state.

3   And on an operating table in a National Zoo research center in Front Royal, VA, a clouded leopard, already near extinction in Southeast Asia, is put to sleep while veterinarians collect a vial of his sperm. If samples of healthy clouded leopard sperm can be preserved, some specimens of the living animal probably can be, too.

4   But saving specimens in the laboratory is no alternative to the conservation of species in the wild. However convincingly simple it may appear, the idea that we can save endangered species by taking them into cryo-protection overlooks the forces that are driving them into extinction in the first place: habitat loss, the illegal wildlife trade, poaching[6] and climate change. The giant panda is not endangered simply because its numbers are low. Its numbers are low because logging, farming and the pressure of human development have consumed most of the habitat it needs to survive.

---

[1] *embryo:* unborn animal or human in the very early stages of development
[2] *genetics:* the study of how characteristics are passed on from one generation to the next
[3] *conservation:* the protection of the environment and the natural things in it
[4] *sperm:* cells produced by a male to fertilize a female egg
[5] *Noah's Ark:* in the Bible, the ark was a large boat built by Noah in order to save his family and a male and female of every kind of animal from the Flood.
[6] *poaching:* to illegally catch animals, fish or birds parents to their children

5   The argument in favor of laboratory conservation is compelling, of course. While conservationists have won a few battles here and there over the past few decades, we are losing the war to save biodiversity. Species are dying at an exceptional pace. For example, fresh water species such as frogs have declined by about 45 percent since 1970. The consensus among biologists is that at least one in five species alive today will be extinct within 30 years. Taking the DNA[7] of these species would allow us to store it against the day when these animals have all but disappeared from the wild.

6   Several academic institutions and zoos are committing major resources to this "Jurassic Park[8]"-style approach to conservation. From the "frozen zoo" at Texas A&M's College of Veterinary Medicine—a research-based zoo that uses artificial insemination[9] and other reproduction techniques to breed endangered species—to the Japanese laboratory that hopes to clone a woolly mammoth from a frozen carcass found in Siberia, a growing army of 21st century Noahs is busily constructing high-tech arks in the hope of reversing the trend toward extinction.

7   But what good is saving endangered animals in the laboratory "ark" if in the end there is no place for them to be "fruitful and multiply"? If the tiger becomes extinct because human beings have converted its natural habitat to other uses, to what "wild" are we going to reintroduce a new generation of test-tube tigers 25 or 50 years from now? And if we are not going to return them to the wild, what's the point? They may entertain a steady stream of visitors to our zoos; attention-getting creatures such as pandas and lions could bring in huge profits for entrepreneurs with private parks. But that would not help conservation.

8   This is not to suggest that genetic research has no place in conservation efforts. It has been used successfully to alleviate inbreeding[10] in specimens born in captivity in protected parks and later returned to the wild, as in the cases of the red wolf and the black-footed ferret,

---

[7] *DNA:* the part of a cell that passes on characteristics from one generation to the next

[8] *Jurassic Park:* a 1993 science-fiction fantasy movie about a theme park with cloned dinosaurs

[9] *artificial insemination:* a method in which male sperm is injected into a female for the purpose of reproduction, commonly used in animal breeding

[10] *inbreeding:* the repeated reproduction of closely related animals or people, can lead to genetic weaknesses

for example. There's no doubt that cryobiology can be an invaluable aid in maintaining genetic diversity among captive populations. The real problems begin, however, when it comes time to set those captive populations free.

9   Even when endangered species can be bred in a laboratory environment, it is rare that they can be successfully reintroduced to their native habitats. Eight out of 10 attempts to reintroduce endangered species to their native habitats have failed. Even the few efforts that are considered successful—the reintroduction of the Arabian Oryx to the desert in Oman, for example, and the golden lion tamarin to the Atlantic coastal rain forest in Brazil—have later developed serious problems. The oryx is again being poached, while the tamarin population, which underwent a hugely expensive effort to reintroduce it, is still suffering as a result of inbreeding. There are only between 100 and 200 of them in the wild today.

10   Even assuming that the factors that cause endangerment can be brought under control in laboratory or protected environments, successful reproduction techniques and returning captive-bred animals to the wild is an expensive, prolonged, and problematic endeavor. The golden lion tamarin conservation program, for example, has spent an estimated $22,000 per surviving animal. Many of the problems with a limited gene pool still remain even though reproduction physiologists have spent much time in preserving animals through laboratory work, or breeding them in zoos. Natural selection[11] no longer applies to animals kept in zoos or artificially bred in captive settings. Having been protected from predators[12] and diseases, these animals have no further part to play in the ongoing drama of evolution. And in the meantime, the human development or other threat that reduced the species in the first place may well have continued, limiting the choice of a suitable habitat.

11   The bottom line is that there are no scientific miracles or quick technological fixes to the problem of biodiversity loss. The only way we can truly save endangered species is by focusing our efforts and our resources on protecting their habitats and preserving the complex ecological functions upon which all species depend. Genetic research

---

[11] *natural selection:* a process where only the animals and plants that are best suited to an environment live and produce young, while others die off. This is how species evolve.
[12] *predators:* animals that hunt and kill other animals

may prove to be a valuable, if limited, tool for conservation. But, in the end, the battle to save endangered species will be won or lost in the field, not in the laboratory.   100

12   Toward the end of the movie "Jurassic Park," the owner of the ruined theme park recalls the trick attractions he created in his youth and says that, all his life, what he most wanted was to create something that was real. Zoos have a very important role to play in educating the public and making it care more about conservation. But unless   105 we can ensure the survival of endangered species in the wild, unless we keep our focus on lands rather than labs, our zoos will be no more representative of nature than movie sets are of reality. The animals we pay to see will be but living illusions—tragic reminders of what we could have saved, but in the end, lost.   110

About the Authors
Eric Dinerstein is chief scientist of the World Wildlife Fund (WWF); Karen Baragona is with WWF's species conservation program.

➤ SUMMARIZING THE MAIN IDEAS

What do you think are the main ideas in the reading "Protecting the Wild"? Skim through this reading once or twice again to get the main ideas. Then write a brief summary of the main ideas below. When you finish compare your summary with a partner's.

_____

_____

_____

➤ VOCABULARY IN CONTEXT

Find each word in the reading (the paragraph is in brackets [ ]). Use context clues to guess the meaning. Write your guess. Compare your answer with some of your classmates' answers. Finally, check the dictionary to see how well you guessed.

Vocabulary	*Your Guess From Context*	*Dictionary Meaning*
1. preserved [1]	_____	_____

2. breakthroughs [1]   _____   _____

3. survival [1]   _____   _____

4. reversing [6]   _____   _____

5. converted [7]   _____   _____

6. alleviate [8]   _____   _____

7. captivity [8]   _____   _____

8. prolonged [10]   _____   _____

9. endeavor [10]   _____   _____

➤ TAKING A CLOSER LOOK

Part A: The Details

Read "Protecting the Wild" again, this time focusing on details. Then answer these questions in your own words. When you finish, discuss the answers with your classmates.

1. Explain the term "cryopreservation."

2. What is the purpose of the project "Noah's Ark"?

3. According to the authors, what are the forces driving endangered species to extinction?

4. Why are biologists concerned about the frog population?

5. What measures are biologists taking to preserve fresh water frogs and other water species from extinction?

6. According to the authors, why is cryopreservation not a practical solution for saving endangered animals? (paragraph 7)

7. According to the authors, what factors make it problematic to return captive-bred animals to the wild? (paragraph 10)

Part B: Making Inferences

Answer these questions by making inferences from the reading.

1. Why do you think the authors are opposed to saving endangered species through laboratory techniques?

2. Do you think the authors like zoos? Why or why not?

3. Do you think the authors are optimistic about conservation measures in the future? Why or why not?

►READING SKILL: Argumentative Writing

Argumentative writing provides support for an author's opinion on an issue that has more than one side. The purpose of argumentative writing is to persuade the reader to agree with the author.

Part A: Evaluating Argumentative Writing

While you may or may not agree with the author's viewpoint, you need to be able to evaluate the argument the author makes in order to judge its strength or validity. A strong argument will contain a *thesis* (the author's viewpoint) based on rational *reasons*. Each reason will be supported by relevant *evidence* such as facts, statistics, and/or examples. In summary, a valid argument is a logical one, based on rational thought, not emotion. In order to evaluate the validity of an argument, take notes or underline the main points as you read.

►READING SKILL PRACTICE: Evaluating Argumentative Writing

Read these notes taken from the main points of argument in the reading "Protecting the Wild"

Points

Thesis: The battle to save endangered species will be won or lost in the wild, not in the laboratory.

Reason 1: Saving endangered species by taking them into cryo-protective custody ignores the forces that are driving species into extinction such as: habitat loss, the illegal wildlife trade, poaching, and climate change. (paragraph 4)

Evidence: The giant panda is not endangered simply because its numbers are low. Its numbers are low because logging, farming, and other forms of human development have taken over their habitat.

Reason 2: Even when endangered species can be bred in a laboratory environment, it is rare that they can be successfully reintroduced to their native habitats. (paragraph 9)

Evidence: Eight out of 10 attempts to reintroduce endangered species to their native habitats have failed. Even the few efforts that are considered successful—the reintroduction of the Arabian Oryx to the desert in Oman, for example, and the golden lion tamarin to the Atlantic coastal rain forest in Brazil—have later developed serious problems.

Reason 3: Even assuming that the factors that cause endangerment can be brought under control, returning captive-bred animals to the wild is an expensive, prolonged, and problematic endeavor. (paragraph 10)

Evidence: The golden lion tamarin conservation program has spent an estimated $22,000 per surviving animal. (expensive)

Evidence: Many of the problems with a limited gene pool still remain even though reproduction physiologists have spent much time in preserving animals through laboratory work or breeding them in zoos. (prolonged)

Evidence: Natural selection no longer applies to animals kept in zoos or artificially bred in captive settings. Having been protected from predators and diseases, these animals are no longer part of evolution. (problematic)

Now evaluate the strength of the argument.

Your Evaluation

  1. The reasons are:

      a. _____ rational

      b. _____ emotional

  2. The evidence is:

      a. _____ relevant

      b. _____ not relevant

3. The authors' thesis, based on the reasons is:

   a. _____ valid

   b. _____ not valid

4. Do you agree with the viewpoint of the authors?

   a. _____ yes

   b. _____ no

   c. _____ undecided

Part B: Reliability of Sources

As well as examining the validity of the argument the author makes, you should also check on the reliability of the sources the author uses and/or the author's qualifications and expertise in the subject area. Usually this information appears at the end of an essay or news article.

➤ READING SKILL PRACTICE: Reliability of Sources

Read the information about the authors at the end of Reading One. Do you think the authors of this essay have the expertise to write about this issue? Why or why not?

➤ INTERACTIVE JOURNAL RESPONSE

Choose one of these questions and write a response. Be prepared to give an oral summary.

1. What do you think of cyropreservation as a conservation measure?

2. The authors claim, "The only way we can truly save endangered species is by focusing our efforts and our resources on protecting their habitats and preserving the complex ecological functions upon which all species depend." What do you think can be done to help people recognize the value of saving habitats?

3. Investigate research and recovery efforts for one endangered animal and report on it.

READING TWO

➤ **BEFORE YOU BEGIN**

1. From the title of Reading Two, what issue do you think will be discussed?

2. Now skim the first and last paragraphs in the reading. What position on the issue do you think the author takes?

➤ **AS YOU READ**

Skim "Lift the Ban on Ivory" to get an idea of what it is about.

LIFT THE BAN ON IVORY

1   The prosperity of Homo sapiens in the future depends on how well we preserve the planet's ecological systems now. Through careful and responsible use of our natural resources, we can insure a better environment in which future generations will be able to prosper. One major way to accomplish this will be to preserve biodiversity. The protection of biodiversity will require sustainable wildlife management techniques that are consistent with local cultural customs and assure the survival of wildlife species while still allowing for their utilization. Sustainable wildlife management is especially important in Africa where trade in ivory has long been a controversy.

2   Although the situation seems to have become grave in recent years, the killing of elephants for their ivory by humans is well documented throughout history. As far back as the 7th century BC, hunting for ivory caused the near extinction of elephants in Western Asia, and the numbers in India have been steadily declining over the

last millennium. In West Africa, recorded declines in the population   25
resulted from the Arabian ivory trade in the 17th century. It was,
however, during the Colonial era[1] in the 1800s, with settlement
expansion and the introduction of modern technology, in particular
high-powered rifles, that elephants began to come under increasing
threat throughout various regions in Africa. By the 1980s, poaching   30
and ivory smuggling[2] was out of control right across continental
Africa. Elephants were being killed at the rate of 60,000 per year.

3   Due to the growing demand for ivory, the elephant population in
Africa halved from an estimated 1.3 million in 1979 to around 600,000
in 1989. That year the Convention on International Trade in   35
Endangered Species (CITES) banned all trade in ivory, and the elephant
population has since stabilized—in some countries even increased.

4   In 1997, CITES lifted the ivory ban for the southern African states
of Namibia, Botswana, and Zimbabwe—where the elephant population had actually increased—to allow them to hold onetime auc-   40
tions[3] of their existing stockpiles[4] of ivory, despite much protest
from animal rights activists and environmental groups. At CITES
2000, the trade debate eventually came to a compromise which was
basically "no ivory trade for now." The decision to ban the trade of
ivory may please Western environmentalists, however, it is only   45
increasing the environmental problems and creating greater poverty
in many African countries.

5   Environmentalists and wildlife organizations, mainly from the
Western world, are campaigning for a total ban on all ivory trade.
They believe that any legal or "controlled" ivory trade will lead to   50
uncontrolled poaching and the extinction of the African elephant.
The southern African states of Namibia, Botswana, Zimbabwe, and
South Africa disagree, arguing "controlled" ivory trade should be
resumed. They believe that conservation through utilization is the
most effective way to manage and conserve the elephant population   55
while at the same allowing the local people to survive. They give two
important reasons to support their position.

6   The first reason is there are now simply too many elephants for
the available habitat. In Kruger National Park in South Africa, for

---

[1] *Colonial era*: period when Europeans controlled Africa and settled in various parts of it
[2] *smuggling*: illegally taking goods, animals or people out of a country
[3] *auctions*: a public sale where goods are sold to the person offering the highest price
[4] *stockpiles*: large quantities stored for future use

example, you cannot drive two minutes without coming across an   60
elephant. And usually it is more like 100 or 200 elephants, ambling
along. The last cull[5] took place in 1994, and since then elephant
numbers have swelled to almost 9,000 from 7,500 inside the park
alone.

7   "Elephants are the world's largest land mammals, and they have   65
big appetites," says Chris Styles, deputy director of the Rhino and
Elephant Foundation, a South African conservation organization.
Styles supports culling as a way of both managing wildlife and of
keeping the population in check. "Some weigh as much as six tons
and require too much space to be allowed to multiply unchecked on   70
a poor continent facing pressure from the human population," he
explains.

8   Hwange Game Park in Zimbabwe provides more evidence of
elephant overpopulation. The Department of National Parks there
has calculated that Hwange already has twice as many elephants as   75
it can sustain. With international scrutiny[6] in mind, in 1994 it
obtained an independent review from the environmental department
of Price Waterhouse, an independent auditing company, to verify
their population surveys. In the final analysis a cull was recom-
mended. But culling is expensive and unless Zimbabwe can sell the   80
ivory and hides on the international market, culling will not be cost-
effective.

9   Africa is a developing continent with an expanding population of
humans. Africans understand the complexity of the issue but they
also realize the very real need to strike a proper balance between   85
conservation and the requirements of a growing human population.

10   The second reason offered by those supporting sustainable management of the elephant herds is that the human population in Africa
suffers from extreme poverty. Much of the African population
subsists on less than a single dollar a day. Environmentalists in the   90
West argue that protecting elephants and other wildlife will benefit
the poor through tourism. But although tourism brings in a substantial
amount of money each year, the majority of this money never ends
up with the poor in local villages where it is needed the most. Rural
farmers rarely, if ever, reap the benefits of tourism, yet they are the   95

[5] *cull:* a planned killing of animals in a group or herd in order to reduce their numbers
[6] *scrutiny:* close examination

ones that have had to give up land for the wildlife reserves and protected parkland where the elephants roam.

11   Originally, in Zimbabwe as in other countries in Africa, indigenous people lived alongside elephants and other wild animals, carrying out subsistence[7] hunting for meat and using hides and ivory to trade.   100
But through colonization, the best land was given to the colonists, with the more marginal regions being designated as wildlife reserves, leaving only the arid[8] regions next to the wilderness areas for the indigenous people to struggle upon.

12   Peasants on this land adjoining national parks now share it with   105
some 18 percent of the country's 70,000 elephants, as well as other wildlife. And as can be imagined, it is a less than a harmonious existence. They wrest subsistence crops from the arid soil, only to find the crops trampled by elephants, which also often destroy huts and too often kill humans in the process. Not only have the peasants   110
been forced off the best land, but through the wildlife preservation schemes they have also been prevented from utilizing wildlife in the traditional way.

13   The majority of Africans argue that the goal of conserving wildlife can best be achieved through utilization. When it comes to elephants   115
and the ivory trade, many are in favor of culling and lifting the ban on the ivory trade. The more humans can benefit from wildlife, the more incentive they have to conserve the environment. As rural farmers in Africa begin to accumulate economic gains from wildlife, it will be in their own interest to preserve that same wildlife. Only in   120
this way, can there be a true paradigm shift from the desire to eliminate wildlife to the desire to foster its growth.

---

[7] *subsistence:* taking only what is needed for survival
[8] *arid:* dry

➤ SUMMARIZING THE MAIN IDEAS

What do you think are the main ideas in "Lift the Ban on Ivory"? Skim this reading once or twice again to get the main ideas. Then write a brief summary of the reading below. When you finish, compare your summary with a partner's.

_____

_____

_____

➤ VOCABULARY IN CONTEXT

Find each word in the reading (the paragraph is in brackets [ ]). Use context clues to guess the meaning. Write your guess. Compare your answer with some of your classmates' answers. Finally, check the dictionary to see how well you guessed.

Vocabulary	*Your Guess From Context*	*Dictionary Meaning*
1. utilization [1]	_____	_____
2. grave [2]	_____	_____
3. stabilized [3]	_____	_____
4. compromise [4]	_____	_____
5. resumed [5]	_____	_____
6. reap [10]	_____	_____
7. designated [11]	_____	_____
8. incentive [13]	_____	_____

➤ TAKING A CLOSER LOOK

Part A: The Details

Read "Lift the Ban on Ivory" again, focusing on details. Then answer these questions in your own words. When you finish, discuss the answers with your classmates.

1. How far back in history has the trade in ivory been documented?

2. What two factors brought about the biggest threat to elephants in Africa during the 1800s?

3. What happened to the elephant population in Africa between 1979 and 1989?

4. What measure was taken in 1989 to protect the elephant population? How successful was it?

5. What reason do environmentalists give for wanting a total ban on the ivory trade?

6. Which countries are in favor of lifting the ban on the ivory trade?

7. According to the reading, why is culling not a realistic approach to managing the elephant population in Zimbabwe?

8. Why are rural farmers not benefiting from tourism in many African countries?

Part B: Making Inferences

Answer these questions by making inferences from the reading.

1. Which side of the argument do you think the author of this article takes?

2. Do you think the author is optimistic about the co-existence of humans and wildlife in Africa? Find support for your answer in the reading.

►READING SKILL: Evaluating Argumentative Writing

To evaluate the validity of an argument, take notes or mark the main points as you read. The following question guideline will help you.

Question Guideline for Evaluating Argumentative Writing

- What is the author's thesis?

- What reasons does the author provide in support of the thesis?

- Are the reasons based on rational thought, or emotion?

- What kind of evidence is given?

- Is the evidence relevant—directly connected to the reasons the author presents?

- Does the information come from reliable sources?

➤ READING SKILL PRACTICE: Evaluating Argumentative Writing

Part A: Your Notes

Thesis: _____

Reason 1: _____

Evidence: _____

_____

Reason 2: _____

Evidence: _____

_____

Part B: Your Evaluation

Evaluate the argument by answering these questions.

1. In your own words, write a one-sentence statement of the author's thesis.

   _____

2. The author's thesis is supported by reasons that are mostly:

   a. _____ rational

   b. _____ emotional

3. The evidence is:

   a. _____ relevant

   b. _____ not relevant

4. The author's thesis is:

   a. _____ valid

   b. _____ not valid

5. The sources of information are:

   a. _____ reliable

   b. _____ not reliable

➤ COMMUNICATE

Which side of the argument do you agree with in Reading Two: the argument made by Western environmentalists, or the argument made by African governments? Prepare evidence (from the article or other sources) to support your viewpoint. Then discuss your viewpoint with a partner. Your teacher may ask you to work with someone who holds the opposite viewpoint so that you can argue your side.

Use the expressions from the Appendix on page 212 to help you.

➤ INTERACTIVE JOURNAL RESPONSE

Choose one of these questions and write a response. Be prepared to give an oral summary.

1. According to the article, many Africans believe that the more humans can benefit from wildlife, the more incentive they have to conserve the environment. Which approach to conservation does this refer to? Do you agree with this approach? Why or why not?

2. The idea behind utilization is that natural resources are used on a sustainable level while yielding economic benefits to the local people. Are there any examples of this approach being carried out in your country? Explain.

3. Are you optimistic about the ability of humans to manage and protect nature for the future? Why or why not?

THE FINAL FRONTIER

Before the Wright brothers, people did not believe that human flight was possible. Before the Spirit of St. Louis crossed the Atlantic, people did not believe they could travel around the world by air. People's beliefs about what is possible have changed. Today, low Earth orbit travel is possible for wealthy individuals, and long-range plans include space tourism for people from all nations.

READING ONE

➤ **BEFORE YOU BEGIN**

In this last chapter, you will be reviewing the reading skills that you have learned in this book.

Part A: Warm-up Discussion

1. Consider the title of the article. If necessary, check the meaning of "frontier." What do you suppose the title means?

2. An idiom, "to promise (someone) the moon," is used in this article. What do you think it might mean?

3. Would you like to travel in space? Why or why not?

Part B: Reading Pace

In Unit 1 you learned that 800 words a minute is a good reading pace for general comprehension. You have been practicing skimming and skipping unknown words while searching for the main ideas. Give yourself 90 seconds to skim "The Final Frontier." Without slowing down, use a pencil to:

1. Circle the title and underline the first and last sentences of the first paragraph.

2. Underline the first sentence of each body paragraph.

3. Underline the last sentence of the article.

4. Based on your skimming, what seems to be the main topic of the reading?

    a. _____ It is not likely that space tourism will ever be popular.

    b. _____ It is very expensive to travel in space.

    c. _____ Space tourism is a probable trend in the future.

➤ **AS YOU READ**

Read "The Final Frontier" again a little more slowly. Look for the main ideas.

THE FINAL FRONTIER
by DC Agle, from *Hemispheres*

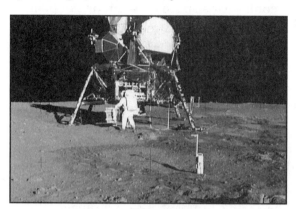

1   Since the beginning of time, salesmen have been "promising their customers the moon" but it wasn't until 1969 that someone actually made a sale. 1969 was the year that Neil Armstrong and Buzz Aldrin took humanity's first steps onto another world. Such a monumental moment in history captured global attention. That year, in a strategy that was part spirit of the times and part publicity stunt[1], Pan American World Airways began selling memberships to its First Moon Flights Club. A $5 deposit reserved one of the first seats on a commercial shuttle flight to the moon. There was one problem: No commercial space vehicles were in production or even on the drawing board of any serious rocket scientist. What happened with the First Moon Flights Club should have made the entire travel industry take notice. More than 93,000 would-be lunar tourists signed up, providing Pan Am with an unexpected half a million 1969 dollars. Three decades later, no airline has yet booked round-trip passages to the moon, or into space, for that matter. But, says Buzz Aldrin, what was once the realm of science fiction movies and advertising stunts is becoming reality. Aldrin, now an advocate of space commercialization, foresees a new world out every tourist's window.

2   "Privatization will make it possible for an average citizen to travel into space," says Aldrin. "Space tourism is a big market that, once it takes off, will grow quickly. And when that happens it will reduce the cost tremendously."

3   Aldrin is not alone in his desire to open the final frontier for the average person. Supporting him are several other former astronauts, as well as many rocket scientists, businessmen, and starstruck[2] advocacy groups[3].

---

[1] *publicity stunt:* something done only to get attention

[2] *starstruck:* enthusiastic, fascinated

[3] *advocacy group:* group which supports a special interest, such as space tourism

4   "There already is a space tourism industry" says Patrick Collins, a guest researcher for Japan's National Space Development Agency. "Each year, over 10 million people visit a space museum or camp, an aerospace research and development center, or a rocket launch facility. It is a business already estimated to be worth more than $1 billion annually. But beyond present-day terrestrial space tourism (tourism on earth, about the topic of space), the general public has an enormous unsatisfied desire to travel into space, and there are large profits to be made. We have market studies that tell us so, and not only from the United States and Japan but Canada and Germany as well."

5   Collins' studies revealed that over 70 percent of the people surveyed under the age of 50 would be interested in taking an exo-atmospheric—that is, outside of the earth's atmosphere—pilgrimage. But getting surveyees to put their money where their mouth is[4] has always been a problem, so even Collins was shocked with his findings in that respect. His research showed that over 30 percent of US respondents and 50 percent of Japanese would be willing to part with up to three months' salary for a shot at space, even if their off-planet time was measured in hours or even minutes and not days or weeks. Of that 30 percent, 10-20 percent said they would be willing to part with six months' pay, and 5 very determined percent claimed they were willing to pay an entire year's salary for the experience—for many Americans, that's about the same amount they would pay to an adventure guide to climb Mount Everest.

6   Who are these people and why are they willing to part with such large sums? Buzz Aldrin knows. "They are the adventure tourists paying $60,000 to travel in a submersible[5] to the see the Titanic. They are flying private jets around the world and climbing the world's tallest mountains. Why? They do it because adventure is adrenaline[6]-generating. They know what it is to be part of something new and different, and when they return from space they will be a different person. Maybe not because of what they've seen but in the eyes of other people. And that uniqueness is something that people want."

7   What the people want, and are willing to pay for, could be very profitable for business. Based on the survey in Japan and several

[4] *put their money where their mouth is (idiom)*: show they mean what they say by spending money
[5] *submersible*: an underwater vehicle, a personal submarine
[6] *adrenaline-generating*: exciting

other studies, a University of Berlin researcher estimated that even at a "service price" of $50,000 per ticket, the space tourism market could quickly grow into a $60 billion-per-annum market. "It would become bigger than the satellite market, which is currently the biggest source of revenue for the commercial space industry," adds Aldrin. 70

8   While the Japanese government sponsored the studies, it is not the only bureaucratic entity looking into space tourism. NASA has been cooperating with the private Space Transportation Association's efforts to build a Space Travel and Tourism Division. Also making the dream a reality is the Federal Aviation Administration, which is preparing for the day when it will have to certify and regulate all traffic as it rockets from US airspace to outer space and back. 75 80

9   Though space tourism visionaries are happy to talk about research studies and bureaucratic red tape, the question they most often hear is "So when can I go?" The answer is that it depends on what potential space tourists are looking for. If you want a trip to one of the planned space hotel/casinos, estimates vary from seven to 25 years down the road. If all you need is a taste of space, then get your money out—the ride of your life is possible. The world's first space tourist, multi-millionaire Dennis Tito of California, paid $20 million for his journey to the International Space Station. His week in space was successfully completed on May 6, 2001. 85 90

10   Those willing to hold out for the seven to 25 years for the orbiting hotel/casino will find that their future vacation spot will have been well-planned. At least two multinational design firms are doing the groundwork on the first hotels in space. Allowing for a low-cost reusable launch vehicle and high volume, such a trip could cost as little as $20,000. Whether choosing a "hop" to the International Space Station, or waiting for a Ritz in orbit, the question remains, "Can average people really do this?" After all, since 1961, space has been a place only for specially-trained and athletic astronauts. But "normal people can absolutely do this," says Aldrin. "We have amusement parks filled with rides that are much more stressful than many forces you feel in space." 95 100

11   But will space tourists ever get to fulfill their dream of seeing the sunrise glinting off the crater Tycho or hitting a golf ball in the Frau 105

Mauro Highlands like Apollo astronaut Alan Shepard? Hilton International seems to think so. Hilton recently hired renowned architect Peter Inston to design a Lunar Hilton. So far, the Britain-based lodging company has invested $300,000 in search of just the right combination of glass domes, galactic viewing ports, and one-sixth   110 gravity sport facilities for humanity's first lunar hotel.

12   One wonders: When that inevitable day arrives and the first lunar tourists exit their lodging to stand amongst the still-pristine[7] footprints left by the Apollo astronauts, what will they be thinking? Apollo 12 commander Charles "Pete" Conrad Jr. provides one possible answer.   115 "Perhaps they'll feel the same as tourists of today who venture to Valley Forge[8] and see where some of the battles were fought. But what is really important is that by people being there, it means we have truly opened up our neck of the woods[9] for commercialization. And that means that the explorers of the world will have gone out   120 into space even farther."

---

[7] *pristine:* fresh, as if new

[8] *Valley Forge:* the site of a series of battles during the American Revolutionary War. These battles marked the shift towards victory of the Americans over the British.

[9] *neck of the woods (idiom):* neighborhood, local area

➤ CONTEXTUAL PARAPHRASING

In Unit 2, you learned to guess the meaning of unknown words by noticing "contextual paraphrasing", signaled by the punctuation of commas, dashes, and parentheses. These sentences from the article use contextual paraphrasing. Circle the word being defined, and underline the definition.

1. But beyond present-day terrestrial space tourism (tourism on Earth, about the topic of space), the general public has an enormous unsatisfied desire to travel into space. . . . (paragraph 4)

2. . . . over 70 percent of the people surveyed under the age of 50 would be interested in taking an exo-atmospheric—that is, outside of the Earth's atmosphere—pilgrimage. (paragraph 5)

➤ VOCABULARY IN CONTEXT

Find each word in the reading (the paragraph is in brackets [ ]). Use context clues to guess the meaning. Write your guess. Compare your answer with some of your classmates' answers. Finally, check the dictionary to see how well you guessed.

Vocabulary	*Your Guess From Context*	*Dictionary Meaning*
1. advocate [1]		
2. foresees [1]		
3. pilgrimage [5]		
4. part with [5]		
5. entity [8]		
6. groundwork [10]		

➤ SCANNING FOR DETAILS

Unit 3 focused on the reading skill of scanning. Scanning means moving your eyes quickly down the page looking for specific information such as facts, names, dates, and other details.

Scan the reading quickly to find answers to these questions. Using your own words, write a complete sentence to answer each one. When you finish, discuss the answers with your classmates.

1. What was the "First Moon Flights Club"?

   _____

   _____

2. When was it started?

   _____

3. How many people signed up for the First Moon Flights Club membership?

   _____

4. What did Collins' research show about American and Japanese people's interest in space tourism?

_____

_____

5. According to Buzz Aldrin, why are adventure tourists willing to pay so much money for space tourism?

_____

_____

6. There are many different groups of people interested in space tourism. What are the groups mentioned in paragraphs 3 and 8?

_____

_____

7. When will tourists be able to stay at a space hotel?

_____

_____

8. What company believes that it will be possible to develop tourism on the moon in the future?

_____

_____

➤ MAKING INFERENCES

In Unit 7 you learned how to make inferences about a writer's deeper or implied meaning. Answer these questions by making inferences from the reading.

1. Judging from the context, what is the meaning of "would-be lunar tourists" (paragraph 1)?

2. Why was Collins surprised by the results of his survey? (Refer to paragraph 5.)

3. Read the final paragraph again. Apollo 12 commander Conrad imagines that the first tourists to the moon will feel the same as the American tourists who visit Valley Forge. Why does he make this comparison?

➤ SIGNAL WORDS

In Unit 5 you learned about signal words:

- Words that signal change (yet, but, although, however, despite, while)

- Words that signal more (such as, in addition, as well as, also, and, moreover, for instance, furthermore, for example).

Read these sentences taken from the article. Circle the signal word and underline the new information the writer is giving or the new point he is making.

1. Since the beginning of time, salesmen have been "promising their customers the moon" but it wasn't until 1969 that someone actually made a sale.

2. Supporting him are several other former astronauts, as well as many rocket scientists, businessmen, and starstruck advocacy groups.

3. NASA has been cooperating with the private Space Transportation Association's efforts to build a Space Travel and Tourism Division. Also making the dream a reality is the Federal Aviation Administration.

4. Although space tourism visionaries are happy to talk about research studies and bureaucratic red tape, the question they most often hear is "So when can I go?"

➤ PARAPHRASING

As you learned in Unit 9, paraphrasing means using your own words to express the meaning of a sentence. This is done by using simple vocabulary and changing the grammar.

Part A

Choose the paraphrase which most closely matches the original meaning.

1. Such a monumental moment in history captured global attention.

   In other words,

   a. _____ Long ago, people's attention was kept by monumental moments.

   b. _____ Around the world, people noticed this important historical moment.

   c. _____ Such a heavy time long ago kept the global community waiting.

2. That year, in a strategy that was part spirit of the times and part publicity stunt, Pan American World Airways began selling memberships to its First Moon Flights Club.

    a. _____ That year, Pan American World Airways started to sell First Moon Flights Club memberships as an advertising gimmick which also caught the spirit of the times.

    b. _____ That year, using a spiritual stunt for publicity, Pan American World Airways began selling memberships to its First Moon Flights Club.

    c. _____ In order to sell the spirit of the times to members and play the public game, Pan American World Airways that year began using a strategy of the First Moon Flights Club.

Part B

Paraphrase these sentences from the reading. Use your own words by replacing difficult vocabulary, and changing the grammar.

1. Aldrin, now an advocate of space commercialization, foresees a new world out every tourist's window.

    _____

    _____

2. But getting surveyees to put their money where their mouth is has always been a problem.

    _____

    _____

➤ TEXT MAPPING

In Unit 8, you learned how to make a text map. Text mapping is a way to outline and take notes. A good text map can help you understand and remember the main points of an article.

"The Final Frontier" has no sub-headings. You need to find the main ideas by skimming:

- Skim the article and choose the main ideas from the list below.

- Then choose the most important details in each part of the article to fill in the text map.

Main ideas:

- Recent market studies on space travel

- Interest in space tourism since 1969

- Space tourism possibilities, now and future

Details:

- 30% of Americans would pay 3 months salary for a space trip

- 1969 First Moon Flights Club

- first suborbital trip was completed May 6, 2001

- bureaucratic support for market studies: Japanese government, NASA, Space Transportation Association, Federal Aviation Administration

- terrestrial space tourism industry - space museums, aerospace research centers, rocket launch

- space hotel—in 7 to 25 years—$20,000

- Hilton International designing a space hotel

Text Map

Topic: Space Tourism

1. _____

-
-

2. _____

-
-

3. _____

-
-
-

➤ SUMMARIZING THE MAIN IDEAS

In Units 4 and 10, you learned to read for the main ideas and to summarize them. Using your text map, write a brief summary of the main ideas of "The Final Frontier." When you finish, compare your summary with a partner's (about 100 words).

_____

_____

_____

_____

_____

 ►COMMUNICATE

This list includes the global topics that you have read about in this textbook.

1. Scan the list and rank each issue from 1–12, according to two criteria: Ranking A is how important or interesting the topic is *to you* personally (how it affects your life), and Ranking B is how important you think the topic is *to the world*. 1 is most important, 12 is least important. You may want to look back at earlier chapters in the textbook to help you review the topics.

Ranking A Importance to Me Personally	*Ranking B* Importance to the World	*Global Topic*
_____	_____	Millennial Generation
_____	_____	Cultural Differences
_____	_____	Lifestyle Choices
_____	_____	Aging
_____	_____	Youth in Action
_____	_____	Music
_____	_____	Work
_____	_____	Inequality
_____	_____	Wisdom
_____	_____	Endangered Languages
_____	_____	Managing Nature
_____	_____	Space Tourism

2. When you have finished the ranking, look at the topics which you have marked number one for you personally and for the world. Take ten minutes and write some notes about why you marked them number one.

3. Find a partner and discuss your choices with him or her.

Use the expressions from the Appendix on pages 211–213 to help you.

➤ INTERACTIVE JOURNAL RESPONSE

Choose one of these questions and write a response. Be prepared to give an oral summary.

1. Dennis Tito paid 20 million dollars to be the first space tourist in April 2001. He said, "There's a spiritual aspect of it—to be off the planet Earth and looking back at the Earth. I have been on this Earth for 60 years; it's about time I get off and look at where I have lived all these years." Would you like to have this experience? Why or why not?

2. Do you think there are any disadvantages to space research and space travel?

3. What is the most adventurous thing you have ever done? Why did you do it? Did you enjoy it?

APPENDIX—USEFUL EXPRESSIONS

Asking Opinions (Units 1, 2, 5, 12)

Do you think . . . ?

What do you think about . . .[verb + ing] . . . ?

How about you?

What's your opinion of . . . ?

Which one did you [choose/rank as #1/like best] . . . ?

Expressing Opinions (Units 1, 2, 3, 5, 6, 8, 11, 12)

In my/our opinion . . .

As far as I'm concerned . . .

It seems to me that . . .

From my point of view . . .

I/we believe that . . .

I/we think it's important to . . .

Reporting Opinions (Units 1, 5, 6)

[John] said that he agreed . . ..

In [John's] opinion . . .

She thinks that . . .

Agreeing (Units 2, 5, 6, 7, 11, 12)

That's right.

I think so too.

I completely agree with you.

I agree.

Disagreeing (Units 2, 5, 6, 7, 11, 12)

I disagree.

That's true, but . . .

Yes, but don't you think . . .

I see your point, but . . .

I see what you mean, but . . .

I'm afraid I don't agree with you because . . .

Giving Reasons (Units 2, 3, 6, 7, 8, 11, 12)

I/we have [3] reasons for my/our opinion.

The first (second, final) reason is . . .

Another reason is . . .

Brainstorming (Unit 4)

How (what) about this:

Let's try . . .

Here's an idea. . .

I wonder if . . . ?

Responding to Ideas (Unit 4)

What about this idea for an ending?

How about saying . . . ?

Let's say . . .

I'm not sure that will work.

Active Listening (Units 9, 10)

1. Nonverbal

   Nodding, smiling, eye contact

2. Short Responses to Show You're Listening

   I see. Really? Oh? Mmmm. Yes.

   Did you? Were you? Didn't you?

3. Asking Follow-up Questions

   What did you do then?

   What happened then?

   How did you feel?

   Did you learn anything from this experience?

Storytelling (Unit 10)

1. Introducing Your Story

   I'd like to tell you about what happened when I [played "fighting crickets" with my father/my son.]

2. Showing Time Order

   First, next, then, finally

   A few minutes later . . .

3. Concluding

   After this happened, I felt . . .

   I learned . . .

Expressing One's Values (Units 2, 7, 12)

I don't believe in [verb + ing]. . .

I value . . .

[noun] is [not] important to me.

[verb + ing] is [not] important to me.

I don't eat meat because . . .

Summarizing Your Results to the Class (Unit 7)

During our discussion, we decided that . . .

To summarize our discussion, we agreed that . . .

All of us think/believe/feel/prefer . . .

Most of us . . .

Some of us thought . . . while others thought . . .

TEXT CREDITS

PHOTO CREDITS

Page 1, Charlein C. Sheets/ Getty Images. **Page 13,** Michael Doolittle/ The Image Works. **Page 15,** Joe Sohm/ The Image Works. **Page 33,** Monika Graff/ The Image Works. **Page 41,** Sonda Dawes/ The Image Works. **Page 49,** Tom Stewart/ Corbis. **Page 67,** Mario Tama/ Getty Images. **Page 76,** AP/ Wide World Photos. **Page 85,** Spencer Platt/ Getty Images. **Page 94,** Vasily Bekrodimitris/ AP/ Wide World Photos. **Page 103,** Bill Lai/ The Image Works. **Page 105,** Alan Carey/ The Image Works. **Page 127,** Skjold/ The Image Works. **Page 137,** Grameen Bank. **Page 147,** Bill Bachman/ The Image Works. **Page 155,** Rachel Epstein/ The Image Works. **Page 161,** Ketkar/ DPA/ The Image Works. **Page 170,** J. H. Robinson/ Photo Researchers. **Page 179,** Tyler Hicks/ Liaison/ Getty Images. **Page 189,** Howard Burditt/ Reuters/ Getty Images. **Page 197,** Courtesy of NASA. **Page 199,** Courtesy of NASA.